W9-BYZ-817

Henry Close, ThM

Becoming a Forgiving Person
A Pastoral Perspective

Pre-publication
REVIEWS,
COMMENTARIES,
EVALUATIONS . . .

"**I** do not know anyone with more knowledge as a therapist and clinical trainer who could write a better book than Henry Close. His wide range of experiences and thoughtful reflections on forgiveness are rich resources of wisdom. I've used many of his suggestions on how to help people struggling with issues of unforgiveness. Readers will long remember his stories and practical insights on this troublesome subject."

Burrell D. Dinkins, ThD
Johnson Professor
of Pastoral Counseling,
Asbury Theological Seminary,
Orlando, Florida

"**E**xtraordinarily user-friendly, this book dismantles offenses and forgiveness into thoughtful and thought-provoking segments. Close uses stories and examples to create deeper understandings of emotional pain and of offenders. This is not as much 'how to' as it is examples of better ways."

Betty Alice Erickson, MS, LPC, LMFT
Therapist in Private Practice,
Dallas, Texas

"**B**ecoming A Forgiving Person is a tender and compelling work which charts differing paths that lead to personal healing through the medium of forgiveness. Close's wisdom of psyche and soul come together in very practical ways through his myriad stories and illustrations."

Virginia Felder, MDiv, ThM, DMin
Licensed Professional Counselor,
Licensed Marriage and Family Therapist,
Tucker, Georgia

More pre-publication
REVIEWS, COMMENTARIES, EVALUATIONS . . .

"With *Becoming a Forgiving Person,* Henry Close has written a timely, personal, and practical guide to the challenging problem of forgiveness. He discusses his own struggles with forgiveness, emphasizing that forgiveness is much more than a technique, that indeed 'serious forgiveness often requires fundamental changes in our lives.'

What I find genuinely insightful is his recognition that by refusing to forgive, we actually imprison ourselves. He enriches his personal account of difficulty in forgiving with narratives of others who have been able to forgive. The book is down-to-earth, practical, and useful. There are many reasons to add this book to your collection. I strongly recommend it!"

David Barstow
Pastoral Psychotherapist
and Editor/Publisher
of *Pilgrimage: Reflections
on the Human Journey*

"In a warm and inviting manner, Henry Close invites the reader to consider the meaning and possibility of forgiveness in our interpersonal relations. The book draws on the insights of psychology as well as the experiences disclosed in a long and fruitful pastoral counseling career. Close also reflects upon a crucial experience of the need to forgive in his own life. In a creative conjoining of religious and psychological insight, the book explores the dynamics of being hurt, the struggle to live in forgiveness, and the strategies and tactics of forgiving. Readers find themselves both enlightened and motivated to deal with broken relationships. We are taught about forgiveness and led to forgive."

C. Benton Kline, ThM, PhD
Professor of Theology
and President Emeritus,
Columbia Theological Seminary

The Haworth Pastoral Press®
An Imprint of The Haworth Press, Inc.
New York • London • Oxford

Becoming a Forgiving Person
A Pastoral Perspective

Becoming a Forgiving Person
A Pastoral Perspective

Henry Close, ThM

The Haworth Pastoral Press®
An Imprint of The Haworth Press, Inc.
New York • London • Oxford

Published by

The Haworth Pastoral Press®, an imprint of The Haworth Press, Inc., 10 Alice Street, Binghamton, NY 13904-1580.

PUBLISHER'S NOTE
Identities and circumstances of individuals discussed in this book have been changed to protect confidentiality.

Cover design by Jennifer Gaska.

Library of Congress Cataloging-in-Publication Data

Close, Henry T., Th.M.
   Becoming a forgiving person : a pastoral perspective / Henry Close.
      p. cm.
   Includes bibliographical references.
     ISBN 0-7890-1855-1 (alk. paper)—ISBN 0-7890-1856-X (pbk. : alk. paper)
     1. Forgiveness—Religious aspects—Christianity. I. Title.
BV4647.F55C58 2004
234'.5—dc21

                                            2003006682

This book is dedicated
with affection and respect
to my friends and colleagues,
Jenny Felder and Wade Huie

ABOUT THE AUTHOR

Henry Close, ThM, is a respected leader and innovator in pastoral counseling. He is a member of the American Association of Pastoral Counselors and a retired clinical member of the American Association for Marriage and Family Therapy. He taught in Columbia Seminary's doctoral program and has led many seminars in his field. He has written over fifty professional articles. His book *Metaphor in Psychotherapy* was a 1999 selection of the Behavioral Science Book Club and the Psychotherapy Book Club. He has had a keen interest in forgiveness throughout his professional life.

CONTENTS

Acknowledgments

No one has ever accused me of being well organized about anything, so it was with much trepidation that I decided to write about such a complex topic as forgiveness. Fortunately I had a friend and mentor, Barbara Thompson, who pushed me to be better organized, and offered many thoughtful suggestions. My friend Wade Huie also read an early draft of the manuscript. His feedback was extremely valuable.

Special thanks to Burrell Dinkins, whose input has enriched many of the things I have written. Thanks also to Jenny Felder, whose love, support, and wisdom have been immensely valuable. Her sister Mimi also read and commented helpfully on this manuscript. I am especially grateful to Peg Marr and Karen Fisher, my patient and forgiving editors at The Haworth Press. Their suggestions have made this a better book.

Thanks also to you my clients, whom I cannot mention by name. You let me be a part of your lives for a while, pushed some of my own growing edges, and stimulated my thinking. You have taught me about the struggle to forgive, and to become a more forgiving person. Some of you have forgiven horrendous things. I am a better person for having been part of those processes.

I take confidentiality seriously, and have made every effort to protect your identity. Most of the time, I think that even you would not recognize yourself. All identifying details have been changed.

Some of the material in this book came from other writers whose names I have forgotten. I read your material long ago, long before I ever thought about writing a book myself, and I did not keep adequate notes. Please forgive me.

Many of the vignettes I describe are compilations of two or more incidents. Some of the stories are partly fictional for dramatic emphasis. I have chosen these stories for their emotional and spiritual truth, which is ultimately what is important.

Thanks to the following publishers who graciously allowed me to use material from their books: J. P. Tarcher, an imprint of Penguin Putnam Inc., Harcourt, Paulist Press, Christian Century Foundation, Washington Square Press, HarperCollins, Impact Publishers, Zondervan Publishers, and Beacon Press.

Preface

Bless those who persecute you.

St. Paul (Romans 12:14)

Repay no one evil for evil.

St. Paul (Romans 12:17)

Anyone can entertain a new idea; the exceptional person can be changed by a new idea.

Some years ago, one of my daughters was mugged on her way home from work. She managed to fight off the assailant, but in the process, she ended up with a gash across the top of her head and a broken arm.

Among other things, I was interested in my reaction. It wasn't exactly anger. It was much deeper than that. It was a profound loathing, hatred of this person who hurt my little girl. She was thirty years old, but to me she was still Daddy's little girl. I think I could gladly have killed him. I think that in some ways I had a harder time of it than my daughter did. I was very, very disturbed at her being victimized.

She told me later that the intensity of my reaction was supportive to her. It conveyed to her a deep quality of caring, and seemed to give her a kind of security in a world that had suddenly become very insecure. I wondered if it also may have meant to her that since I reacted so strongly, she didn't have to. She could turn the hatred over to me (I had enough for both of us, with plenty left over), and she could devote her energies to dealing with her trauma.

I mentioned this incident later to a group of young therapists I was supervising. One of the women in the group said she found my reaction very comforting—that a man would not excuse another man for his violence. I'm sure some of you have suffered worse things than my daughter, or have had loved ones who have, and your reaction may have been similar to mine. I think that's important. A person who has been victimized needs to hear your rage, your indignation that somebody could treat another human being so cruelly.

But alongside the reality of hating when someone is cruel to our loved ones are the disturbing words of Jesus. "You have heard that it was said, 'You shall love your neighbor and hate your enemy.' But I say to you, love your enemies and pray for those who persecute you, so that you may be children of your Father who is in heaven." (Matthew 5:43f) "Lord how often shall my brother sin against me, and I forgive him? As many as seven times?" . . . "Not . . . seven times, but seventy times seven." (Matthew 18:21, 22) "Forgive us our debts, As we also have forgiven our debtors." (Matthew 6:12) "[I]f you do not forgive men their trespasses, neither will you Father forgive your trespasses." (Matthew 6:15). Or those profoundly disturbing words from the cross, "Father, forgive them . . ." (Luke 23:34)—words that let us know he was serious about forgiveness, that he really meant those things that he said.

How do we put these two things together: the reality of a very basic reaction to a child who is injured, and the importance of forgiveness? If we forgive an assailant, will not our daughters believe that we do not care, that we are indifferent to their humiliation and suffering? How can we support them in their trauma, how can we surround them with what strength we have, if we seem indifferent? How do we handle these two realities: the deep and bitter—and important— resentment toward someone who hurts our children, and those strange and troubling words of Him whom we call Lord and Master, to forgive, to love our enemies? How do we forgive when it really counts?

This book represents part of my struggle to cope with this dilemma.

Before writing this preface, I reread the text. I was embarrassed at some of the things I had written about myself that sounded like whining. I'm sure that is partly an accurate portrayal. I did sometimes exaggerate my reactions for dramatic effect, in a kind of literary license, but I'm really not as neurotic as I sound in these pages, or at least not quite as neurotic.

In this book, I want to discuss forgiveness as an option, not a demand. I think it is to one's advantage to forgive, and I am offering some understandings that may make that easier. There are stages to go through, and sometimes painful realities must be faced. Beginning the processes of forgiveness is a choice that only you can make.

PART I: INTRODUCTION—
WHY I AM INTERESTED
IN FORGIVENESS

It is better to light one small candle than to curse the darkness.

(Chinese proverb)

I have been interested in forgiveness all my professional life. As an imperfect human being living in an imperfect world, I face challenges every day to accept and to practice forgiveness. As a marriage and family therapist, I see the importance of forgiveness for personal growth and for healing in relationships. It has certainly been a recurring theme in my own family.

As a pastoral counselor, I recognize forgiveness as one of the foundations of my spiritual tradition, reflecting the nature of God, as I understand God. If I can forgive, I can lay aside the burden of resentment, and direct my energies toward the future. When I forgive, I feel my own spirituality more deeply.

As one concerned for social justice, I know the central place of forgiveness—and its power—in the work of Mohandas K. Gandhi and Martin Luther King Jr. More recently, Desmond Tutu's program of truth and reconciliation has sought to bring forgiveness and healing to South Africa. It is significant that nonviolent protest has been effective only in cultures that emphasize fair play. Jews were nonviolent in Nazi Germany, and were engulfed in the Holocaust.

This is not primarily a book about technique, the quick fix, promising that if you do such and such, you will be able to forgive easily. Technical answers do not call for fundamental changes in the inner self, but forgiveness often does. No matter how much we would like to be able to forgive another and then go on with life as usual, serious forgiveness often requires fundamental changes in our lives. It does not easily fall within the framework of technique.

Instead, this is a book about becoming a forgiving person, cultivating a style of life that is conducive to forgiveness. It is about basing our lives on deeper levels of the psyche, where there are alternatives to guilt and blame. As forgiving persons, we can refrain from taking offense at trivia and can even survive catastrophic injury.

I don't think it is necessary to be religious to forgive someone, but I do think of forgiveness as being deeply spiritual.

The world in which we live is oriented in many ways to blaming. An obvious example is the radio talk show. Typically, the host angrily proclaims that all of life's problems are "out there," somebody else's fault. For Utopia to arrive, these other people (institutions, political parties, and so forth) need to change and be like the host.

Similar themes run through many movies and TV shows. An innocent saintly victim is cruelly oppressed by the evil villain. As we witness the injustice of this, we become indignant or enraged. We easily identify with the victim. When finally the hero avenges the victim's suffering, we feel an inner satisfaction, elation, at the revenge. We gloat at the villain's humiliation and/or suffering. This is a dominant theme of many movies—especially the action movies. Contrast this with shows that meaningfully portray forgiveness. They are few and far between.

Revenge sells better than forgiveness.

We often approach relationships—even with spouses and children—from an adversarial, competitive stance. We tend to think the proper way to influence someone is by intimidation—sometimes physical, sometimes emotional or rational. Many people can simply out-argue others. Even religion is sometimes used to intimidate or shame other people.

An adversarial attitude toward life is oriented to winning, not forgiving. When we forgive, we seek peace and healing in a relationship. Forgiveness is oriented to the future. When we blame, we focus on the past. We are more concerned about justifying our anger than about forgiving. There is therefore much cursing of the darkness.

When we are in a blaming mood, we are not very interested in being forgiven either. We want to be exonerated, not forgiven. We rationalize our faults, and want others to recognize that whatever we did was justified.

Because forgiveness represents complex realities, you may leave this book with as many questions as answers, but I hope you will also have a deeper sense of peace. I hope you will find it easier to live with other people, and they will find it easier to live with you.

Chapter 1

The Dilemma: How Could I Forgive a Friend Who Betrayed Me?

Don't get mad; get even.

Love your enemies and pray for those who persecute use you.

Jesus (Matthew 5:44)

Some years ago, a colleague and friend was injured in an auto accident and unable to work for several months. When he was ready to resume his practice, he asked me if I would lend him money for a new car.

I had no problem with that. Alexander was a good friend, and I had recently inherited some assets as part of my father's estate. I borrowed against these assets to lend the money to my friend. He signed a note, agreeing to repay me with the same interest I was paying on my loan.

Six months later, Alexander declared bankruptcy. I was not concerned. Our transaction was based on friendship, not business.

Two years later, his practice was thriving and he was making more money than I was. I asked him to begin repaying the loan. I was aghast when he said that the bankruptcy had annulled that obligation. Today, he has more assets than I do, yet feels no responsibility for honoring his commitments to me.

How could I ever forgive such a betrayal? How could I ever get past my hurt and anger, and see him as anything other than an enemy?

As time went by, my resentment grew, but it also became more and more of a burden. I wanted to be free of it. I wanted to be able to look at this person casually, without constantly thinking of his betrayal. I wanted to be able to lie down at night and not have my thoughts and feelings drawn to it. I wanted to be able to go to sleep feeling something other than resentment. As long as I was obsessed, I was still the victim. I wanted to be free.

I remembered a client whose husband had had a brief affair with his secretary. When my client, Mary, accidentally found out about it, she was at first devastated and then irate. Nothing her husband said or did made the slightest difference. She was determined to punish him for what he had done to her.

They started marriage therapy with me shortly after Mary learned about the affair, and I saw them for several weeks. I was as ineffective as the husband in tapping into anything but her indignation. This woman, although a bit touchy, had once been relatively cheerful and altruistic. She had now become cold and cruel. She isolated herself from her friends. She was always tired and began to develop physical problems that I am sure were stress related.

Mary had to have revenge, but had no idea what that entailed or how to achieve it—or what it would accomplish. The betrayal was always in her mind, no matter what distractions she sought. The obsession was taking a terrible toll on her and her family emotionally, physically, and spiritually.

This is not an unusual reaction to a serious offense. The movie *Dead Man Walking* is about a man who kidnapped, raped, and terrorized a young woman, Debbie Morris. He had also killed another young woman.

When Debbie met the parents of the other young woman, she was disturbed by the bitterness that consumed them.

> Seeing the effects of their abiding anger and hatred had helped convince me I needed to let go of those feelings myself. As weird as this may seem, I doubted I would have ever tried to forgive Robert Willie if it hadn't been for my unsettling exposure to such an all-consuming bitterness. (Morris, 1998, pp. 179-180)

I did not want to become like Mary, or like the parents of the murder victim. The truth is that I wasn't sure I was all that different.

I thought back on some of the offenses against me that I have resented. I vividly remember a girl in my high school class teasing me about being skinny. It was years before I could think of that without cringing. A classmate in college threatened to beat me up over some minor offense that I don't even remember. A colleague ridiculed a very personal article I had written about my reaction to a friend's suicide. By any objective standard, these were trivial offenses, yet I reacted with some of the same resentment as I had to my friend's betrayal.

When I realized my hurt and angry feelings were not going to dissipate by themselves, I began to wonder what steps I could take to find healing. I wanted to move on, and that meant I would have to forgive him. But what would that entail, and how would I do it?

I thought of people who have suffered catastrophic injury. Wars are often scenes of unthinkable brutality: children are forced to kill their parents; mothers are forced to watch as their babies are murdered; little girls have their hands chopped off.

Compared to events such as those, losing a friend and a few thousand dollars was utterly trivial. That understanding, however, did not enable me to forgive.

I have read of people who actually have forgiven terrible offenses. One woman's daughter was raped and killed. The mother went to the prison to offer her forgiveness to the killer (Bristol, 1982). Another woman was so filled with rage and contempt for the man who had killed her daughter that she had asked to witness his execution. Then one night she wrote to him. The words seemed to flow from her pen. She told him that she forgave him and was willing to visit him. "The instant the letter was in the mailbox, all the anger, all the rage, all the lust for revenge disappeared" (van Biema, 1999, p. 58).

Still, the possibility of my writing Alexander to say that I forgave him was utterly unthinkable to me.

During a war in Armenia, a young nurse's family was murdered and she was abducted to serve as a sex slave for a brutal army officer. After months of abuse she escaped, and eventually worked as a nurse in a field hospital. One day, this officer was admitted for injuries sustained in battle. The nurse provided the intensive care he needed to recover (Augsburger, 1996).

Somehow these acts of forgiveness did not seem relevant to me.

I remembered times when people have forgiven *me,* sometimes for serious offenses, yet that was not enough to enable me to forgive. At times in the past I have been able to forgive other people. Whatever enabled me to do it then did not seem applicable here, or was not available to me.

I like to think of myself as a forgiving person. It is one of the values I try to live by. It is also central to my work as a therapist. I frequently tell clients it is in their best interests to forgive. So I sincerely wanted to put this principle into practice in my own life. I wanted to be able to forgive Alexander, but the situation made that extremely difficult. He acted as though there was nothing to forgive, as though something was wrong with me for making an issue of it. That attitude was itself an offense.

It was clear that he would never apologize to me. He would never change. So if I were to forgive him and get on with my life, I would have to find the resources within my own psyche. I would have to be the one who changed.

How could I do that? How could I begin the journey of forgiveness?

PART II: OFFENSES—THE WAYS IN WHICH WE ARE HURT

After I got past the initial hurt and shock of Alexander's betrayal, I tried to reflect on the situation, and in particular on the ways I had been hurt. I realized that I had been abused in at least three different areas. First, Alexander offended against my freedom. I could have made good use of the money he took. I felt blocked, constricted. Second, he offended against my self-esteem. He treated me with contempt, implying that I was unworthy of being treated decently. I felt humiliated. Finally, he offended against my capacity for intimacy. He violated my trust, my closeness to him as a friend. For a while, I was hesitant to trust anyone. I felt betrayed (see Appendix B for an elaboration of this framework). Perhaps all offenses are like this. They primarily offend us in one area, but other areas are also involved.

A father promises to meet his young daughter for an evening, but does not come. First, he has caused her the inconvenience of getting ready and then having nowhere to go (an offense against freedom). Second, he has told her by his behavior that she is not worthy of his time and attention (an offense against self-esteem). Third, he has violated her trust and left her desolate (an offense against intimacy).

If this is an isolated act, it is a minor offense. When it happens repeatedly, it becomes catastrophic. An *act* of indifference is trivial; a *stance* of indifference can be devastating. No matter how benign the father's intentions, or how justified his reasons, his behavior is a betrayal. He injures his child.

Chapter 2

Offenses Against Freedom:
My Choices Are Limited

> If anyone strikes you on the right cheek, turn to him the other also.

Jesus (Matthew 5:39)

It had been a long hot day. The air conditioner in my car was not working and it seemed that every car in the city of Atlanta had congregated in my neighborhood. As I inched forward in the left turn lane, somebody suddenly cut in front of me. I hit the brakes so hard that my car stalled. I fumed as I waited for the light to change again, entertaining all kinds of vicious fantasies of revenge. This was about the time I was beginning to conceive this book, so the event was, as they say, grist for the mill.

I asked myself first if something this trivial was worthy of discussion. From my own reactions in situations such as these, and from the reactions I have seen and heard about from others, this is not trivial. So many people have been killed for traffic offenses that the term "road rage" has entered our vocabulary.

It was not the inconvenience per se that annoyed me so much. It was the implication that the rules that applied to ordinary mortals such as me didn't apply to this driver. From that perspective, it was also an offense against self-esteem.

If I thought this person had accidentally gotten in the wrong lane and then *asked* me for the right of way, I would gladly have done so. Apparently this driver just didn't want to wait in a long line, as I had been doing, and felt entitled to push me out of the way.

I no longer think this was a deliberate offense, although it felt that way for a while. That was just this person's way of being in the world—at least on this occasion.

In that situation, this driver had a kind of power over me by limiting my freedom, my sense of being in control of my own life. In response, I wanted to have power over this driver, to put this person down, but I was a stranger, and I would never see this rude individual again. Even if I had known the person, I doubt that I would have said anything. I would not have wanted to reveal that I got upset over something so "trivial."

I must confess one fantasy: a little later in the same day, on a deserted road, I imagined finding this person who had just had an accident and was asking for help. I would offer my assistance (magnanimous of me, no?), but announce that I recognized the driver as the one who had cut in front of me so rudely.

When Adam was killed in the crash of a private plane, he left a wife, two small children, and not enough insurance. Darlene had to go to work to try to maintain the standard of living that Adam had provided. She did not want to subject her children to any more changes.

It took her four months to find a suitable job, but she was very happy in it. She enjoyed the work, which provided opportunity for advancement. After a year or so, a new manager took over her branch of the company. A powerful, charismatic man, he immediately took charge of everything. He also tried to take charge of everyone—including Darlene. When she rebuffed his sexual advances, he began making life very difficult for her. She got the hardest jobs; she had to work unreasonable overtime; everything she did was criticized.

Darlene thought about reporting this sexual harassment, but she knew nobody would intervene, and would be even more difficult for her. She thought about quitting, but she needed the money. She also knew her boss would sabotage any efforts in that direction by giving her bad references. As with so many other women in the workplace, she was trapped. To continue working in that situation was intolerable, yet there seemed to be no alternative.

A similar situation involved a man in training to be a psychiatrist. This kind of training is often very stressful for the family, and his wife wanted to see a therapist. The young man naively referred her to his supervisor. A few months later, he discovered that this therapist had become sexually involved with his wife. He had persuaded her that it was "for her own good."

The young trainee was trapped. If he did nothing, he would watch his marriage disintegrate. If he reported it, the supervisor would deny it, accusing the trainee of some neurotic reaction to the process of supervision. If he quit, he would be branded a failure.

Many times the situation is even worse. Poverty forces many people—perhaps a majority of the people in the world—into virtual slavery. Men suffer brutal abuse from their overseers. Women are held in slavery as prostitutes. Children toil in sweatshops and have no chance to be children.

Such incidents are at least offenses against our freedom. Someone has a certain kind of power over us, and abuses it. These offenses range from inconveniences such as a traffic offense, to acts of oppression such as sexual harassment, to enslavement. To some degree, we are left with a sense of helplessness. More than anything else in the world at that moment, we want once again to be in control. We want not to be helpless.

Probably most offenses against freedom also offend by implication against our self-esteem. They imply that we are not entitled to be treated with decency and courtesy. Alexander certainly did this to me when he stole money from me. But the overt act is an offense against freedom.

The wish to be in control of my life is not some casual whim. Part of my sense of being a person comes from an ability to be in charge of my own life and my world, at least to some significant extent.

I can think of times when I have been angry—furious even—about not being able to control my physical world. A key won't open a door, I spill oil while adding it to my car, a shoelace breaks, I can't find my appointment book. People have even been known to beat their cars if they won't start.

At least I haven't done that.

I especially want to be able to have some influence—power—over the people around me. At the very least, I want people to notice me. If I am standing on a street corner, I expect people not to bump into me. If I say "Hello" to someone, I expect some kind of response. I want, I *need,* to have that kind of personal power.

I see it also when I try to persuade someone to take my point of view seriously. Its validity is so obvious to me. Anybody with a grain of sense should see things my way, or at least consider that my perspective has validity. When I cannot make the other person take my point of view seriously, I feel very frustrated. Why can't I influence him or her? Am I that insignificant?

When people are thoroughly frustrated, they stop communicating altogether. They simply exchange proclamations (and accusations). This seems to be especially true in regard to politics and religion.

All of us want to be taken seriously. We want to have power *with* people. If we cannot have power *with* people, it is then that we try to get power *over* people.

Chapter 3

Offenses Against Self-Esteem: I Feel Humiliated

Never attribute to malice something that might simply be accidental or stupid.

My doctor is almost always late for appointments. So when I go there, I set aside plenty of time and take along things to do—a crossword puzzle, a book, and so forth. With these preparations, I really don't mind waiting.

One day, Dr. Cohen was quite late. One of the other patients, who had arrived after I did, was irate. I heard him complain angrily to the receptionist, "Nobody keeps me waiting!"

Another thing I do while waiting is observe other people.

I found out later that this was a powerful businessman, belligerent and narcissistic to everyone. For him, being kept waiting was not an inconvenience, it was an insult. His self-esteem was at stake.

He was, in effect, looking for self-esteem in the waiting room. He wanted to be recognized as an important person. But waiting rooms are not oriented toward providing or affirming self-esteem. Neither are highways; the rude driver taught me that.

A brash, impulsive teenager pulled into the parking area outside a convenience store. He carelessly flung open the door of his car and put a tiny scratch on the adjacent car. Unfortunately, the scratched car was the owner's pride and joy, a holy shrine that he kept in mint condition. He was irate at the tiny scratch and demanded that the offending driver apologize.

The careless driver accused the owner of making a mountain out of a molehill and refused to apologize. The owner would not back down. The conflict escalated, an altercation erupted, and the young driver was killed.

We men seem to be particularly sensitive to offenses against our self-esteem—put-downs. We tend to be thin-skinned; it is often incredibly difficult for us to lose face gracefully.

A major delusion afflicts us men: "If I am to be loved, I must first be admired and respected. If you don't look up to me, you cannot possibly like me. If you do not respect me, you cannot possibly love me."

I am sure that women suffer from comparable delusions, but I don't have the same grasp of them that I do of men's delusions. After all, I have an insider's view of the man thing.

We men present to the world a list of our achievements and virtues. Those virtues and achievements are different for each person: strength, looks, money, brilliance, humor, and so forth. We religious people sometimes find status in showing the world how "spiritual" we are.

Those of us who are therapists sometimes find status in showing off how honest we can be about ourselves and our imperfections. That is better than finding status by intimidating someone, but the concern for status is ever present—to some degree—in everything we men do.

I see this in myself when I remember things I have done that I regret. I tend to hassle myself more for the times I have made a fool of myself than for times when I have treated someone shabbily. In other words, I am more upset when I have compromised my image than when I have compromised my integrity. It is easier for me to rationalize one rather than the other. I think this holds true for most men.

I think this concern for status explains why we resent suggestions. In many places in the world, for instance, it would be unthinkable for a woman to suggest that her sexual partner wear a condom as protection against AIDS. That suggestion would be an insult, implying that the man should have thought of it himself.

It is difficult for us men to admit that we made a mistake, or that we did something stupid or petty, or to accept someone else's interpretation of our behavior. It is extremely difficult for us to apologize, especially to those whose love we want the most, or to admit that we have been hurt by a loved one's rejection. It is tough for us to trust or to love someone—such as a wife—who knows we are not wonderful.

A friend commented on how stressful it was for her to ask for support and nurture. She seldom did, for fear of being turned down. For me, it would have been different. I would be afraid of making a fool of myself. She was thinking in terms of relationships. I, as with most men, would think in terms of status.

In marital conflicts, men and women offend each other differently. The sources of the conflict may be unclear, but the pattern is predictable, and each person tends to punctuate the sequence differently. "Husband withdraws, therefore wife criticizes," or, "Wife criticizes, therefore husband withdraws." The wife's criticism is an offense against self-esteem. The husband's withdrawal is an offense against intimacy. Perhaps this is the origin of the conundrum about the irresistible force meeting the immovable object.

When a man is criticized, he tends to de-importance the critic. After all, the only ones who can damage our self-esteem are those who are important to us. When he does this, the woman experiences it as rejection, and sets out aggressively to reestablish the contact, often by criticizing. The conflict then escalates predictably.

My friend Burrell Dinkins says that when a man has an extra-marital affair, he is looking not for a bed, but for a pedestal. He wants someone who will worship him—a requirement the wife has often ceased to provide.

Conversely, when a woman has an affair, the "sexual" organ she is seeking is not a penis, but an ear. She wants someone who will listen to her—something her husband may no longer do, especially if she has stopped worshipping him.

Some years ago, I was in a therapy group. During one session we were discussing men's concern about status. One thoughtful young man said he finally realized that the people who liked him could care less about his successes. They liked him for things that were absolutely unrelated to status. When he tried to get them to look up to him, to admire him, that interfered with their liking him! If they envied him, they would like him less. But it was a struggle for him to settle for being liked, which he could not control, rather than trying to be admired, which to some extent he could control.

We then talked about how important it was for people to think well of us. We especially wanted the group leader, Alice, to think well of us. One very wise woman commented, "I know Alice *loves* me, so I don't care what she *thinks* about me."

This is in contrast to the way we men think: if you don't think well of me, you cannot possibly like me, much less love me.

I used to believe that it was possible for us men to outgrow this obsession with status. I no longer think that. All we can do is shift the focus of our concern. It is better to find status by being loving and gentle than to seek status by being arrogant and intimidating.

An important foundation of forgiveness is a thick skin. This has not always been considered a virtue. In many cultures, avenging an insult is a badge of masculinity. A teenager who has been insulted may be challenged by his buddies: "Are you going to let him get away with that?"

This is called "defending one's honor." According to this mentality, when a man has been offended, when he has "lost face," his honor, his respect has been challenged. He feels a kind of moral obligation to avenge the offense. If he has been put down, he must put the other person down so the two of them can be equal.

Various cultures handle these situations differently. A Prussian might challenge one to a duel. Brazilian men have been known to kill their girlfriends for dishonoring them, for example, by flirting with another man. A young Arab man murdered his sister because she had disgraced the family by telling the police she had been raped. (Beyer/Amman, 1999).

When people forgive, they are often afraid others will think they are weak. That can be a significant deterrent to people overly concerned with self-esteem.

Parents often offend against their children's self-esteem without even being aware of what they are doing. They use shame as a means of control. Instead of communicating to the child, "What you did was unacceptable," they communicate, "You are a bad person. You should be ashamed of yourself!" or, "I'm ashamed of you!" or, "How can you treat me that way after all I've done for you?" or even, "Do you want Jesus to be ashamed of you?"

I have heard many people talk about such painful experiences. Nothing they ever did was good enough. Nothing elicited the warm smile of affection and approval.

There is a difference between insult and criticism. *Insult* is a direct challenge to self-esteem, usually malicious. Most of us react to insult with hostility and a wish to get even. Criticism *erodes* self-esteem, leaving us feeling defensive and inadequate. Insult is usually obvious. Criticism can be so subtle that we do not always recognize it. We are only left with the vague sense of malaise.

In relation to Alexander, I felt demeaned, humiliated. Forgiving him was going to be difficult.

Chapter 4

Offenses Against Intimacy:
I Have Been Betrayed

The ways of the world are cruel, but human feelings are tender.

C. G. Jung

Perhaps the most painful aspect of Alexander's betrayal was the violation of trust. We had been good friends who greeted each other with warm smiles and affectionate hugs. Conversation came easily, even about things that were very personal. Each of us had supported the other through a period of depression. Each of us was genuinely happy at the other's successes. So when Alexander asked to borrow the money, I was glad to be able to help.

When he refused to pay me back, I couldn't understand it. Had I asked him at a bad time, and he would apologize later? Had I asked in a manner that offended him? Had I misjudged him and our relationship? Certainly I had misjudged the meaning of the loan. For me, it was a personal favor, between friends. For him, it was a business transaction, remote and impersonal.

I told Alexander once, as politely as I could, that his decision not to repay me was causing me considerable distress. I humbly asked him to rethink his position. His reply was a casual, "Henry, get over it!"

I asked him again. "Alexander, please." He said something such as, "It's over and done. Forget it."

I knew if I pursued this, it would become a power struggle that I could not possibly win. His logic was different from mine; his priorities were different from mine. I could not possibly persuade him of the validity of my concerns. The old saying, "It is always easier to make things worse than to make them better," was certainly applicable here. A power struggle would make things worse.

I have enough frustrations in my life already without adding another, but the result was sad. I had lost more than just the money. I had lost a friend. Ultimately, that was what hurt the most.

The serious offenses against freedom and self-esteem are usually sins of *commission*—things someone actually does to us. My friend's betrayal was certainly an example. However, many of the most painful offenses against intimacy are sins of *omission*—things someone has not done.

Mildred was in her early sixties when she was physically disabled. She would have to spend the rest of her life in a nursing home. Mildred was well liked by a number of people. One friend arranged to have some kind of gathering every week in Mildred's room. One week it was a bridge game, the next week a book discussion, and so on. Mildred said this kind of support meant the world to her.

But there was a darkness in her life also. Her daughter Becky, who lived in the same city, practically never visited her. Mildred was at first bewildered by this. Before the disability, she had seen Becky and her children at least once a week. Why was there no contact now?

Then she realized that these get-togethers had always been at Becky's house. Mildred came there, to play with the children, to baby-sit, to help around the house. Now that she could no longer help, Becky initiated no contact with her, and Mildred felt she had been used. She had not been valued for herself, but only for what she could give.

Offenses such as these—even where there has been no malice on the part of the other—are often extremely difficult to forgive.

An essential part of growing up is to forgive one's parents. But forgive them for what? It is usually not specific offenses that are so hard to forgive; it is the whole relationship. It may be difficult to describe, but it is deeply felt.

The children's stance may not be one of overt resentment. It may be a kind of reserve, a holding back, a concealed defensiveness. They give negative interpretations to things the parents say and do. They will not let the parents influence them or define their relationship in any way. Sometimes the children will even be reluctant to accept a gift.

When they are together, there is a guarded quality to the interaction. Eye contact is not warm and engaging, but furtive and elusive.

Conversation tends to be friendly but superficial. Even hugs lack enthusiasm. It may be that no one even knows that something is missing, but at some level they sense the loss.

The parents and the children each want something from the other, but what? Recognition? Apology? It is often difficult for them to put their wishes into words, and so impasses arise and grow, often developing a life of their own.

The reality is that all parents have made mistakes in raising their children. Most parents have made bad mistakes. I certainly have, as did my parents, and as my children will, but if children cannot forgive their parents, much of their own energy for living gets tied up in lingering resentments.

In a marriage also, seemingly inconsequential offenses can lead to horrendous but poorly defined power struggles. When people fall in love and marry, they assume their ways of thinking and living are very similar. Similarities are magnified; differences are minimized and ignored.

But after the honeymoon of the relationship is over, the husband and wife make the horrifying discovery that they are different.

One may be extremely neat, the other sloppy. This is one of the hardest differences to deal with, and can lead to endless power struggles. Each is absolutely convinced that his or her style is correct. Anybody in his or her right mind should know that.

Another frustrating difference concerns the couples' levels of animation. One spouse is a high-maintenance person who insists on a significant degree of activity and stimulating conversation. The other is a low-maintenance person, much more laid back.

When stress is low, it is relatively easy to accept differences, to say to oneself, for instance, "I thought Lee and I were alike in that area. After all, our relationship is based on our similarities. But what Lee did makes me realize we are more different than I thought. I guess I'll have to get used to that."

But if stress is high, it is difficult to be casual about differences. When stress is high enough, one may say to oneself, "I *know* Lee and I are alike in that area. Our relationship is based on our similarities. But what Lee did makes it look as if we are different. I know that can't be, so it must be that Lee is being malicious!"

If stress is high enough, it is actually easier to think of the other as malicious rather than as different. Each will then set out to convert the other to the "right" way of thinking. Because these issues are so difficult to put into words, it is difficult to think of them as needing forgiveness. How do you forgive someone for being different from you, or for not living up to your expectations? Yet that is exactly what is needed.

Impasses such as these have a way of escalating rather than self-correcting. Each person becomes constantly alert to the slightest imperfection in the other. Whenever she says something, he interprets it in the most negative way possible. When he withdraws, she is scathing in her denunciation. They dig at each other over trivia. Each feels the other has betrayed their sacred trust and commitment.

When Martha finally realized that her husband had been sexually involved with her best friend for several months, she was devastated. Her husband had trouble at first understanding why she was so upset. In his opinion, his relationship with the friend was not a threat to the marriage. Why was it such a big deal? The arrangement did not take time or money away from the marriage. He did not regard it as an insult to her. Why was she so upset?

To Martha, marriage meant uniqueness. They were committed to being exclusively important to each other. They shared concerns with each other that they shared with no one else. Their honesty with each other was deeper than with anyone else. Their physical intimacy was uniquely theirs. The affair compromised all of these.

Martha indicated that her husband talking about her to this other person was more hurtful than the sexual infidelity. He and this friend shared secrets that excluded her. She was no longer unique in his life. She had been betrayed by the two most important people in her life.

From Alan's point of view, his affair had been at worst an act of disloyalty, not betrayal: he had minimized the importance of their marriage. From Martha's point of view, it was betrayal. Alan had destroyed something in their relationship and had destroyed something in her. It was for her a catastrophic offense that could not easily be forgiven.

A young woman, a minister's daughter, writes of the crippling aftermath of being raped when she was sixteen.

It is difficult for many to imagine how one's life changes after living through an experience of horror. I cannot imagine how my life might have been had I not been raped. I have little connection to my life prior to the rape. Rape forced me to start over. . . .

I can recall so many firsts since the rape. The first time I felt something other than numb. (I remember . . . how grateful I was for the physical pain to remind me that I was alive. . . .) The first time I wanted to commit suicide. . . . The first time I slept through the night without seeing the dark shadows of a man with arms outstretched walking toward my bed. The first time food actually had a taste to it (three years after the rape). The first time I walked alone outside for a distance of more than twenty feet. . . . The first time I held a man's hand and realized that I could pull away at any time. . . . The first time I looked at my father as Dad, not as a man with the physical capability to commit rape. The first time I looked at myself naked without seeing the fingerprints of the man who raped me all over my body. . . . (Schmidt, 1993)

Catastrophic offenses such as these stir up anxiety in friends and family, and they often say things that are incredibly stupid. One friend told this rape victim, "Why can't you just forgive him and get on with your life?" A minister told her that they would read the Psalms together so that she could understand and accept the meaning of suffering in her life as a Christian. He told her that she would become more ardent in her faith as she learned the value and virtue of suffering.

Incest, similar to rape, is a catastrophic offense in all three areas. In some ways, it is more damaging than rape by a stranger. It is usually not as violent, but it violates a deeper trust. Children trust loved ones to have their best interests at heart and never to exploit their helplessness and vulnerability. Children trust loved ones to love without demanding anything in return.

Although Alexander had not injured me, he had violated a trust I regarded as essential. I did not know whether I could ever forgive him. It certainly was not going to be easy.

PART III:
TRYING TO TAKE CHARGE—
WHAT CONSTITUTES FORGIVENESS

It is not enough to find better answers; we must learn to ask better questions.

Einstein

In contrast to revenge, forgiveness approaches life differently. It has two facets: an inner and an outer. One focuses on my own attitudes and commitments; the other focuses on my relationship with the offender. Both are oriented to the future rather than to the past.

Internally, forgiveness means to renounce revenge of any kind. I will not hurt you. I will not steal from you. I will not humiliate you by spreading malicious gossip. I will not wish you harm. If you are a loved one, I will not punish you by withdrawing. I may end the relationship, but that will be because the relationship is no longer viable; it will not be a kind of punishment. I will not return evil for evil.

Hopefully, I will be able to let go of inner resentments—those ways to punish the image of you I hold in my mind. That is the final fruition of the process of forgiveness. But the first step is to renounce revenge, even if I am still tormented by the injustices I have suffered.

Externally, forgiveness concerns my relationship with the offender (assuming a viable relationship existed). To the extent that it is appropriate, I will look for ways to bring healing to our relationship. I will be willing to take the first step. This does not necessarily mean resuming a relationship. It does mean that I will be open to that possibility *under certain circumstances*. This concept will be more fully explored in a later chapter.

At the time of this writing (summer 2002), the Middle East is being torn apart by conflict. Palestinian terrorists are blowing themselves up to harm Israelis. The Israeli army is oppressing the territory occupied by Palestinians. Each side feels that everything they do is totally justified. Perhaps this is true, but it is clear that the actions of both sides are making things worse rather than better, and the conflict escalates. Winning becomes more important than resolving issues, and the possibility of change becomes more and more remote.

Justification focuses on the past. For those who do that, it is not difficult to justify anything. What is needed is a commitment to the future. This can only happen when people forgive.

Chapter 5

What About Revenge?

Vengeance is mine, I will repay, says the Lord. I will repay.

St. Paul (Romans 12:19)

The pleasure of revenge is in its anticipation.

Ancient proverb

If we live by the principle of an eye for an eye, the world will soon be blind.

Attributed to Gandhi

I knew what it was like to be powerless to forgive . . . . I can only say: however much we have been wronged, however justified our hatred, if we cherish it, it will poison us. It is in forgiving our enemies that we are healed.

Sheila Cassidy, a victim of Chilean torture

My first reaction to Alexander's betrayal was shock. I could not believe he would treat me that way. This feeling soon gave way to anger. When I thought about him, I would mutter curses under my breath. When I was around him, I felt mean and angry. I wanted someone to treat him the same contemptuous way he had treated me. I wanted to get even.

The wish for revenge is very strong in most of us. It expresses a compelling logic that seems to balance the scales of justice. It seems to promise to bring closure to a painful episode and restore our sense of being in control of our lives.

A serious offense upsets our expectations that life will be fair. We are left adrift, confused. The principles by which we make the moment-to-moment decisions of our lives are suddenly threatened. We need something to restore our confidence in the reliability of the world in which we live. We need the security of knowing that we can "get even."

Revenge is also a way of regaining a sense of power. If you have hurt me, you have gained power over me. You have put me down without my consent. Such situations are intolerable for most of us. We want equality.

Revenge is also associated with self-worth. If someone can abuse me with impunity, that implies that I am insignificant, that I have no rights. My suffering doesn't matter. But if some people will stand up for me, will exact some kind of satisfaction from the offender, then my sense of worth as a human being is validated—at least in my own eyes.

The idea of revenge starts out as protective. If you are trying to hurt me, I hope I will be strong enough to make you stop. If I can't stop you, I want to deter you by threatening you with unpleasant consequences—revenge.

However, the wish to get even can sometimes have a benign purpose (although it rarely works out in practice).

Kevin had planned a special evening with his wife. But when evening came, he told her that something had come up, and he had made other plans with his buddies. When she complained, he apologized casually. To Teresa, this was not casual. She needed him to take her seriously. She needed him to know how she felt.

A few days later, they were at a party at his office. About halfway through, she suddenly acted as though he had insulted her, and indignantly walked out.

Kevin was irate. How in the world could she do such a thing?

When he angrily confronted her that evening, she said she didn't know any other way to get his attention, to let him know how much his rejection had hurt her. This led to a major argument that was hurtful to both of them. Teresa's revenge backfired—as it usually does.

Another woman faced a similar situation and handled it differently. Tom and Lillian are recent divorcees in their middle forties, each having left a volatile marriage. After dating each other for a couple of months, they went to a party at Tom's office. He was in a strange mood, and he teased her, bordering on insult. She became more and more angry but did not want to make a scene.

The next day she was faced with four options: she could end their relationship; she could get revenge by criticizing Tom's behavior; she could ignore the incident; or she could *ask* him to change—which would presuppose that she was not seeking revenge, that she had forgiven him. (This reflects the basic ways we humans deal with difficult situations: withdraw, attack, submit. To forgive is somewhat different from all of these.)

To end their relationship would have solved that particular problem, but if one withdraws from all distressing situations, one will soon be totally alone.

If she criticized Tom's behavior, it might have gone something like this.

"What the hell was wrong with you last night?"

"What do you mean?"

"I mean your damn teasing. How could you have treated me that way?"

At this point, Tom would be likely to get defensive. He would say that she is too thin-skinned, or that he didn't mean anything by it, or he was just reacting to something mean she had said earlier. The confrontation would be likely to result in a serious argument.

To ignore it would not help. Tom would have thought Lillian regarded his actions as appropriate and might well have continued such behavior.

Lillian wanted change, not revenge. She commented to Tom, "Tom, I've got a bone to pick with you."

"What's that?"

"At the party last night, you said some really unkind things about me to our friends. I didn't like that; please don't do that again."

If Tom is a relatively normal human being, he will not get defensive, but will apologize and promise not to act that way again. He may even explore some of his own motives for such behavior, but he will never explore his motives if Lillian is critical.

There is no guarantee that this kind of approach will work, although it did for Lillian and Tom. It has a much better chance of success, however, than an angry confrontation. *It is a way of asking a favor rather than making a demand.* It is based on forgiveness, which is oriented to the future, rather than on revenge, which is oriented to the past. It is oriented toward change rather than blame. She is not trying to humiliate Tom; she is asking him to change.

The objection to this kind of approach is that it puts the burden on the victim. Why should Lillian have to be the one to pussyfoot around some insensitive clod such as Tom who deserves to be criticized?

I'm not talking about what is right and appropriate; I'm talking about what is likely to work. If you *ask* rather than demand or threaten, you are more likely to get cooperation rather than grudging compliance. This is strictly a pragmatic point of view. Lillian shouldn't have to bear the burden of Tom's insensitivity. But if she wants him to change, she will forgive.

Some people are able to deal with resentment by a kind of catharsis. It is a form of revenge against the *image* of the person rather than against the real person.

When John was thirteen, his father left the family and divorced his mother. During the next five years, his dad's support of the family was minimal, despite a successful business.

When John graduated with honors from high school, he applied for a college scholarship. The scholarship was denied because his father made too much money. So John asked his dad to pay the tuition. His dad refused, even though he was paying his stepdaughter's tuition.

The only solution for John was to sue to disinherit his father so he could qualify for the scholarship. But he knew that would totally alienate his dad, and end the little support he and his mother did receive from him.

As John understood the deep unfairness of this dilemma, he was at first bewildered, then depressed, then irate. He spent an hour that evening angrily storming around the house, loudly denouncing his dad for his greed and irresponsibility. Finally he quieted down and began thinking with his mother about how to finance his college career. His anger at his father softened to the extent that he could ask for what little help his dad was willing to give.

From one point of view, it was necessary for John to express his anger before he could get past it. Only then could he shift his attention to the practicalities of his situation. From this perspective, anger is like steam in a boiler. These feelings need to be discharged or the pressure will build up to a dangerous level. In fact, colorful displays of anger are often called "letting off steam."

But not everybody needs to express feelings in this way. Many people are simply more reserved (me, for instance). We find our sense of power in different ways. For a long time, I used to hassle myself about that. According to the prevailing pop psychology I needed to express my feelings dramatically, but I just could not do that. I finally understood that it is the deeper realities that are important, not the surface demonstrations.

Nowadays, we don't hear much about the importance of expressing feelings. We have other ways of thinking about life. When John was offended, he felt helpless. When he blew up at the world, he regained a sense of power. From this perspective, it was not the expression of feelings per se that was helpful to him. It was his honesty, his giving himself a sense of strength, his affirmation, "I do not deserve to be treated this way." When he stormed around the house yelling, he no longer felt helpless.

In another situation, a woman was practicing a forgiveness meditation when an image of her father came into her mind. She immediately felt full of resentment and hate, and began stabbing him. Then she said to herself, "This is a safe place to experiment with new feelings. Why not try forgiving?" So she said in her mind, "I forgive you," and all of a sudden an image of her father appeared to her. In it he was sitting there and then started crying. For her, the experience was beautiful and healing.

Was it necessary for her first to experience the anger? Perhaps. Very often, forgiveness lies on the other side of catharsis.

Catharsis sometimes takes other forms. One woman's husband had been abusive to her throughout their married life. He was now dead, but her resentment and indignation toward him remained. She wanted to stop carrying him around in her mind. One day, she spent a couple hours writing an angry letter addressed to him. She detailed the horrible ways he had treated her, and her rage at him. She wrote this letter on what she regarded as appropriate writing material, and then flushed it down the toilet.

Parents sometimes punish their children. Usually the intent is benign. They want to teach their children how to live well in a difficult world. At times, however, parental punishment is little more than revenge.

If a parent has a strong need to be in control, then a child's "disobedience" is a serious matter. It is taken as a challenge to parental authority and must be suppressed. Parents have been known to be emotionally and sometimes physically brutal to their children. "You *will* obey me!" These are words of revenge, not words designed to nurture a child's well-being.

A much happier option is to take children's difficult behavior as challenges to *ingenuity,* not to self-esteem. "How can I elicit their cooperation?" Not "How can I force them to comply?"

A kind of passive revenge is often present in marriages. Husbands are particularly prone to this tactic. A wife criticizes her husband, and to get even, he withdraws. He may leave the house, bury himself in his work or in TV, or get drunk.

In extreme situations, divorce can be a means of revenge. Some revenge probably occurs in every divorce. In some divorces, it seems to be the main ingredient.

If you are considering a divorce, please ask yourself these questions: To what extent am I soberly recognizing that the marriage is not viable? To what extent do I want to punish my spouse for not living up to my expectations? If I forgave my spouse, how would that affect the marriage?

People can also be devious in their ways of getting revenge. The offender may not even know that he or she has been a subject of such revenge. One man described his way of getting even with rude clerks. He would mumble something that sounded kind of like "Thank you very much," but the actual words were an obscene insult, even though the clerk did not realize it. The man was then able to gloat over his triumph.

That struck me as bizarre. This man was taking the clerk's rudeness as a challenge to his self-esteem, as parents sometimes do with children. I much prefer to take rudeness as a challenge to my ingenuity. I will do what I can to establish some kind of rapport with such a clerk. Often, I have gotten a smile and a friendly good-bye. On one occasion, I got an apology, which was much more satisfying than veiled vindictiveness.

Whether I fail or succeed, I feel that I have taken control of my own life. I have not let someone else determine my attitudes.

In relation to Alexander, I wasn't interested in his well-being or in my own ingenuity. I wanted revenge. I wanted to get even.

Finally it occurred to me that I had two ways to get even. I could put him down, so we would be even because we would both be down. Or I could get back up again, so that I would be even no matter what happened to him. That might not be as thrilling as putting him down, but it certainly would be healthier. When I felt once again in control of my own life, revenge would be irrelevant.

George Orwell was a journalist during World War II. On one occasion, he was walking through a recently captured German village with a British officer. They came upon the body of an SS officer by the side of the road. Orwell said that he expected his companion, who had been treated rather badly while a prisoner of the Nazis, to kick the body or spit on it, but the officer simply paused, looked at the body a moment, and walked on.

Suddenly Orwell realized that the idea of revenge is important only when one is oppressed. When one is free, when one is in a position of power, revenge is simply disgusting.

There are at least two fundamental problems with revenge. The first is that revenge easily becomes part of a vicious cycle that has no end. You offend me, and I retaliate. When I retaliate, you are indignant. As far as you are concerned, you didn't do anything to warrant that kind of reaction from me, so you set out to get even with me, and so on and so on. It becomes a kind of game, in which winning is more important than anything else.

When I seek revenge, I am playing your game. We just swap roles back and forth. For the game to end, one of us must apologize and/or forgive, or a third party must intervene, or we must withdraw from each other.

The second problem is that revenge keeps me focused on offenses. As long as this is true, I am still the victim. The offenses still have power over me. I am still living in the past.

Many Jews who survived the Holocaust never recovered. The horrors of that experience were always in their consciousness. They were crippled emotionally. Nothing could ever bring closure, even after emigrating from Germany. It was as though these people brought Hitler with them when they left Germany. Jews who left Hitler behind were much more able to build a new life.

The wish for revenge can be destructive in other areas. Chronic resentment can damage my immune system as well as my judgment and sense of well-being. It can block whatever creative energies I have. It certainly makes me distrustful of other people. As someone once said, "He who seeks revenge digs two graves."

Chapter 6

Is an Apology Necessary?

It is better to be forgiven than to defend your innocence.

During World War II, Klaus Barbie was the Gestapo officer in Lyons, France. Known as the butcher of Lyons, he was unusually brutal to Jewish families.

One evening, a Jewish man heard the police banging on a neighbor's door, and knew that his apartment was next. He hid his wife and two children in a secret compartment, and offered himself to the Nazi officers. He was never to return.

His son, Serge Klarsfeld, was eight years old at the time. Serge survived the war, and married a German woman, Beate. Beate had known nothing of the Holocaust, and was horrified when she realized what her countrymen had done. She embarked on a campaign to expose perpetrators of Nazi crimes—especially Klaus Barbie. Serge and Beate organized a search for Barbie. He was eventually found in Bolivia, and brought back to France for trial.

Barbie showed no remorse for what he had done. He even bragged about the Jews he had killed, saying this was his contribution to the fight against Communism.

Some accused Klarsfeld of simply wanting revenge, but as with most victims, he wanted an apology.

> If Barbie had come back to France of his own accord, said he regretted what he did, said he was young at the time and that he did terrible things, that would have been enough for us. There would have been a trial, but it would have been conducted in an atmosphere of cooperation. In a sense the man himself would have been the judge of the man he used to be forty years ago. (Paris, 1985, p. 129)

This is what the father of Ron Goldman wanted. He was awarded millions of dollars in a civil suit in which O. J. Simpson was found liable for his son's death. Goldman said he would forgo the payment if Simpson would sign a statement admitting that he had committed the murder.

From this perspective, it is the *behaviors* that need to be judged. If the offenders judge them, that is often sufficient. If offenders do not judge their behaviors, if they do not repent, they are still defending who they were and what they did. In that case, another judge becomes necessary.

In South Africa, the Truth and Reconciliation Commission became a forum where victims could tell their stories. Many of these stories were excruciatingly painful, bringing tears to the eyes of judges as well as to others gathered there. But these were times of healing. When people felt they were being taken seriously, their resentment often softened.

A similar movement has surfaced in the American judicial system. Victims have an opportunity to tell their stories in the presence of their offenders. The affirmation and support they feel seems to allow many of them to let go of the past and its resentments—whether or not the offender apologizes—and focus on the future.

An apology from Alexander would have made all the difference in the world to me. It would have meant that he wanted our friendship to be restored, that he no longer saw himself as entitled to stand over me and take advantage of me. He would be renouncing his stance with me. By his behavior, he had put me down, and exploited my naiveté. An apology would be his way of putting himself down, renouncing the power he had in relation to me, as a move toward equality. We could then be even.

All of us step in and out of different mind-sets. When I apologize, I acknowledge this. Part of me committed an offense; another part of me stands in judgment of myself. An apology would have indicated that Alexander rejected the "self" that betrayed me. It would no longer represent his stance with me. But if there is no apology, there is no renunciation of the offending "self."

Various kinds of pseudoapologies actually make forgiveness difficult. A friend may apologize to me because it is the "right" thing to do. I would therefore be obligated to say that everything was all right. This kind of "apology" is often a request to pretend that the offense never happened, or that it didn't matter. It is a wish to feel innocent, not forgiven. It would ask that I not hold him or her responsible.

A true apology has several very clear implications. When I offend against someone, I abuse power. When I apologize, I renounce that power. An apology implies a willingness to accept with grace the fact that the apology may not be accepted. A plumber had a long affair with his wife's sister. When the wife discovered the affair and confronted him, he apologized perfunctorily. She remained cold and aloof, telling him it would take time for her to regain a sense of trust. He was indignant: "I told you I was sorry. What more do you want?" His "apology" was not an apology in the sense that I understand it.

A true apology implies submission to some kind of meaningful judgment and restitution. If this is not the case, then an apology is simply a way of trying to weasel out of responsibility.

If I have criticized you, I must be willing—within the limits of "an eye for an eye"—to be criticized. If I have publicly humiliated you, I must be willing to be equally humiliated in public. If I have stolen, I must be willing to repay with interest. If I have killed, I must be willing to alter my life in ways that will at least partially make up for what I have taken away. This might involve trying to contribute to the world what the victim would have contributed. For instance, a man who killed someone while driving drunk might invest himself in programs for the treatment of alcoholism.

The movie *Gandhi* depicted a terrible time of rioting and killing. A Hindu man came to the Mahatma (a term of respect for a holy man), confessing that he was living in hell because he had killed a Muslim child. Gandhi told him there was way out of his hell. He must find an orphaned Muslim child and raise him as his own—and raise him Muslim.

A true apology implies a willingness to make restitution, otherwise, it is meaningless—pious words. In many cases, the restitution is more important for the one giving it than the one receiving. It is a way of taking one's own faults seriously. Alcoholics Anonymous stresses this as an essential step in the process of recovery.

An apology that points to extenuating circumstances implies that in similar circumstances the offender would behave the same way again. During the Nuremberg trials, most of the Nazis tried to excuse themselves by saying they were merely following orders. This implied that if given similar orders, they would commit the same atrocities all over again.

Many apologies are indirect rather than direct, behavioral rather than verbal. These apologies are often more effective than verbal apologies. The verbal apology is more or less expected, a formality that can be meaningless. In a behavioral apology, I tell you by my behavior that I value you and include you in my circle of friends and loved ones. I do not see myself as entitled to abuse you. I regard us as equals.

An apology certainly makes forgiveness easier, but an apology comes from the offender. In this book, I primarily discuss taking charge of my own life, rather than waiting for someone else to take action. Forgiveness is a way to take charge of my own inner attitudes as well as my behavior—whether the offender apologizes or not. Conversely, to hold resentment is to give up responsibility for my own life.

I knew that Alexander would never apologize to me. If I were to forgive him, I would have to base the forgiveness on characteristics within myself.

Chapter 7

Questions

You should fear those whom you cannot forgive—not for what they can do to you, but for what you thereby do to yourself.

As time went by, I felt—without really understanding how or why—that I was getting closer and closer to being able to forgive Alexander. As I thought about it, several questions came to mind. What would be involved in that forgiveness? Would I have to pretend that I had not been hurt? Would forgiveness be a way of shaming him? Would it mean not holding him accountable, at least in my own mind? Would it mean resuming the relationship as before, as though nothing had happened?

Other people have asked these and other questions about forgiveness. I now had an opportunity to think about them from within my own experience.

I was very familiar with the phrase "forgive and forget." But forget what? I certainly did not want to forget my own naiveté. How could I grow if I forgot my failures? How could I avoid similar mistakes in the future? I also did not want to forget that other people—sometimes even friends—often live by a value system quite different from my own.

The offender is usually the one who admonishes the victim to forgive and forget. He or she wants to resume the relationship without having to apologize meaningfully, without having to take the offense seriously, without having to change. So forgive and forget really means to pretend. "Let's pretend that I did not hurt you. Let's pretend that I am not the kind of person who could have done that. Let me maintain my image of benevolence."

When people say, "Let's forgive and forget!" they may be implying that whatever they did was trivial, and thus, something is wrong with you if you cannot let it go.

However, what an offender wants you to regard as trivial may be anything but trivial in your eyes.

When Clara discovered the family investments had all been liquidated, she was bewildered. Shamefaced, Tony admitted that he had used the money to finance his fanciful dreams of making a fortune. When Clara insisted that he see a therapist, he apologized again, and irritably said nothing was wrong with him. "Why can't she just forgive and forget?"

Forgiving and forgetting can easily lead to a horribly destructive denial. Irene's husband was a seriously abusive alcoholic. Even when he was violent with her and their children, she tried not to get angry. She told herself and the children over and over again, "It's just the booze. He doesn't really mean it. Maybe it's partly our fault. Let's just forget it."

Unfortunately, her children were never able to forgive her for not protecting them. The eldest son would not even come to her funeral.

The appeal of denial is very strong. My first reaction to Alexander's betrayal was something like that. I could not believe he really meant what he said. It was a temporary aberration. Surely he would realize what he had done, and would repay me with apologies. It took a long time to accept the fact that this would never happen.

None of us wants to think of himself or herself as someone whom other people would treat badly. That would undermine our self-esteem.

There is an old saying: "To know all is to forgive all." A deeper understanding of the offender can soften the impact of an offense. Maybe the offender has had a bad day. Maybe he or she does not realize the impact of his or her behavior. Maybe the behavior is motivated more by neediness than by malice. Maybe the offender is driven by demons, inner tormenters, that obliterate any concern for other people. The offender mistreated you, not because you deserve to be mistreated, but because of who he or she is.

All of us are motivated by forces that are somewhat beyond our control. Fortunately, most of those forces are benign, but if we had been exposed to different influences during the formative years of our lives, those forces might be very different.

I have studied World War II extensively. As I have read about the Nazi mentality, which culminated in unspeakable atrocities, I wondered what might have happened if I had been raised in that milieu. I was an impressionable boy, eager to please. I might easily have become one of them. After all, "respectable" people in the history of my own country were often brutal to those they regarded as inferior. Even in the early part of the twentieth century, lynching was sometimes like a kind of community entertainment, attended by women and children. Can anyone confidently say that he or she would have been exempt from the influences that made these conditions possible?

Understanding those issues can be an important ingredient in forgiveness. Even Jesus on the cross prayed for his tormenters' forgiveness on the grounds of understanding. "Father, forgive them, for they know not what they do" (Luke 23:34).

Many think of offenses as challenges. Some even think of them as coming from God, as a way of strengthening one's inner self. Important learnings about oneself can certainly come from any distressing situation. Focusing on them can help one withdraw importance from the offense and invest it into one's own spiritual growth.

Understanding may soften the impact of an offense. But ultimately, forgiveness is based on deeper realities.

Emphasis in contemporary thinking is placed on the rights of the victim and on the accountability of the offender. Offenses are seen as abuses of power, and the responsibility for change lies with the one who has power, not with the victim.

A generation ago, if a man hit his wife, many would have said that she should forgive him, which would mean she should resume their relationship. The mood today is different. Abuse is not viewed as an aberration to be forgiven, but as an injustice to be confronted. Unless the offender takes responsibility for his or her destructive behavior, forgiveness is seen as weak and therefore inappropriate.

From this perspective, the one without power cannot meaningfully forgive. Not until the offender has repented—renounced his or her power—are forgiveness and reconciliation appropriate. This repentance of course implies a willingness to make restitution to the best of one's ability.

I think it is important to distinguish between forgiveness and reconciliation. Forgiveness means to renounce revenge and to be open to healing in the relationship. I don't think there are any circumstances in which this is not appropriate. Reconciliation means to resume a relationship with the offender. In many cases, this is grossly inappropriate.

Frederrick Keene (in an unpublished paper) maintains that New Testament teaching suggests that forgiveness can only be offered by one who has power. As an example, he refers to Jesus on the cross—the epitome of powerlessness. Jesus himself did not offer forgiveness to his killers, but asked God to.

I have trouble with Keene's point of view. The broad thrust of Jesus' teachings is that forgiveness is especially appropriate for the powerless! He was speaking to Jews in a conquered land, who had little power relative to their conquerors. A Roman soldier could compel a citizen to carry his load for a mile. Jesus said to go with him two miles. Jesus said, if someone commandeers your coat, give him your cloak as well, and if someone strikes you on one cheek, turn the other also. "Love your enemies [those who abuse the power they have over you?] and pray for those who persecute you." Or in the words of St. Paul, "repay no one evil for evil."

These teachings were in sharp contrast to the prevailing attitudes of the time: "An eye for an eye, a tooth for a tooth." If offenses are abuses of power—acts that diminish the victim's power—then perhaps all forgiveness must come from a one-down stance.

I see no conflict between accountability and forgiveness. If one truly forgives, one may be in a better position to speak forcibly to the offender. When one forgives, one can seek changes that are oriented to the future, rather than retaliation, which is oriented to the past.

A generation ago, the psychiatrist Frieda Fromm-Reichmann was regarded by many colleagues as a kind of saint.

On one occasion, a patient slapped her during an interview. The patient was immediately horrified at what she had done, and apologized profusely. She then asked if Dr. Fromm-Reichmann resented her.

Dr. Fromm-Reichmann replied that she did not resent the patient per se for slapping her, but like any other human being, she resented being slapped, and she would do what she could to try to avoid being slapped again. However, if she had to give part of her attention to protecting herself, that would take away from her ability to attend fully to the patient's concerns.

The patient solemnly promised that such a thing would never happen again.

This brief incident illustrates several facets of forgiveness. Dr. Fromm-Reichmann did not deny she had been hurt. She held the patient accountable. She made it clear that she would not accept abuse, and that there would be consequences if the abuse continued. She also forgave her: there would be no revenge, and they would continue to work together intimately. Her response expressed the old admonition to "love the sinner but hate the sin."

The patient's reply shows the power of forgiveness to change the offender. But that change is incidental to the purpose of forgiveness. Forgiveness is not a means of manipulation. In forgiving, I take charge of *me*. I do not seek to control you through guilt.

All of us try to influence other people. We want to be taken seriously. We want our wishes and our viewpoints to be respected. In a good relationship, we influence each other easily and openly. In a strained relationship, we often approach each other manipulatively. Inducing guilt is one such approach.

Husbands and wives can be incredibly innovative in making each other feel guilty. "You never . . . (pay attention to me, spend time with me, make me feel loved, and so forth)." Or "You always . . . (expect me to wait on you, criticize me, drink too much, etc.)."

When a spouse induces guilt, both parties lose. One spouse feels coerced into changing; the other never knows whether the changes represent love or guilt. "Do you really want to spend time with me, or are you just trying to get me off your back?"

Parents can also be quite skillful in making their children feel guilty, or the other way around. One elderly woman periodically called her son who lived several hundred miles away. When she was not feeling well, she wanted him to come and spend time with her. When the son pointed out how extremely inconvenient that would be, she would say sadly, "Well, I understand." Needlessly to say, this "forgiveness" effectively controlled the young man.

In intimate relationships, a true forgiveness may be unspoken. For me to say, "I forgive you!" can be haughty and demeaning. In a marriage, for instance, the ideal is to have a balance, an equality, not for one to lord it over the other in any way.

I have a friend—a truly good person—who lost a large part of his retirement to a swindler. He told me that it took a while, but he felt he truly forgave this person. He wanted him to have a good life, but he also felt the man needed to be held accountable for what he had done. My friend testified against him in his criminal trial, and sued him to recover his money.

To me, this makes perfect sense. I don't think I could have done it as gracefully as he, but it expresses the tension between forgiveness and accountability.

True forgiveness is not weakness. After the close of World War II, someone asked Winston Churchill what was ultimately responsible for the war. He said, with his usual flourish, that the malice of the wicked was reinforced by the weakness of the virtuous. Hitler's aggression was "forgiven." It was overlooked, tolerated, rationalized.

If forgiveness means that I will not punish the offender, that presupposes that I have the power to punish. Without that power, the concept of forgiveness is irrelevant.

There are many kinds of punishment. Husbands often punish their wives by withdrawing from them. Or I may punish an offender in my own mind. It can be imaginary as well as real. Inner realities are often more "real" to us than external realities.

I certainly punished Alexander in my imagination for a while. I think that helped me get to the place where I did not need actual vengeance. Those fantasies, however, could easily have developed a life of their own. That would have helped no one, and would certainly have been destructive to my well-being.

I have trouble with the idea that power can be easily perceived or defined. In the abstract perhaps it can, but in the day-to-day functioning of an ongoing relationship, the issues of power are quite ambiguous. Power is not just the capacity to injure someone; it is the capacity to *influence* someone—which is enormously complicated.

A man has beaten his wife, exercising tremendous power over her, but now he suffers an enormous guilt, which she exploits to the hilt. Her threats to leave are terrifying to him. They reinforce his low self-esteem, with its deep feelings of inadequacy and impotence. How can we say that he has the power and she doesn't?

I have often thought that in a disturbed relationship, the *strength* and the *power* belong to different persons. The abuser may have the *strength,* but in many ways the victim may have the power. It often happens in families that the helpless person—such as one who is seriously ill, depressed, or alcoholic—effectively controls the rest of the family through his or her helplessness.

PART IV:
LAYING THE FOUNDATIONS

The significant problems we have cannot be solved at the same level of thinking which created them.

Einstein

For me, forgiving Alexander had two facets. The first was deliberate. I made a commitment to myself that I would not seek revenge. Several times I had the opportunity to bad-mouth him to colleagues. I somehow managed to refrain from doing that.

It took longer for me to forgive inwardly—to get to the place where I could truly wish him well. When I realized that had happened, I began to wonder what had made it possible. What was my inner forgiveness based on? What were its foundations?

Personal growth and maturity take place in two ways. Sometimes it begins outwardly. If I change my behavior, that will influence my inner self. Conversely, if I nurture my inner growth processes, that will change my behavior. To phrase it differently, "Do I become a forgiving person by practicing forgiveness?" or, "Do I forgive because I am a forgiving person?" I am convinced that both are relevant.

Much psychotherapy presupposes that change takes place initially in the inner self. Those changes then express themselves in one's behavior. This approach has been stated very thoughtfully by my friend John Patton (1985) in his book, *Is Human Forgiveness Possible?* He suggests that dealing with shame is the primary basis of forgiveness.

When I am offended, I experience shame. I feel that my sense of self has been damaged. My enthusiasm for living has been impaired. Something vital has been taken away.

Patton's thesis states that healing from the psychic injury is the first priority. When one has dealt with the underlying shame, the energy for maintaining one's hostile or defensive stance around the offender is dissipated. I come to understand that the offender treated me badly because of who he or she is, not because I deserved to be treated that badly. When this happens, then one *discovers* that forgiveness has taken place.

Forgiveness, then, is not something that is initiated; it is an inner healing that one realizes has already taken place. Forgiveness is "discovering . . . that I am more like those who have hurt me than different from them" (Patton, 1985, p. 16).

I think that forgiveness based on healing from shame is probably more true of relationships in which the power is more or less equal, such as between husband and wife. It is not true where power is unequal. It is inconceivable to me that a little girl whose hands had been chopped off by a terrorist would ever think of herself as more similar to him than different from him. She may be able to forgive him some day, but that forgiveness would be based on something quite different than thinking she is similar to him.

The emphasis of this book is different. I am stressing the importance of one's deliberate commitments and behaviors. If I behave differently, I will then come to feel differently and to think differently. Changes in my commitments will change my attitudes toward life. Alcoholics Anonymous expresses this in the saying, "If you don't feel it, fake it!" or "Fake it till you make it!"

This was a major part of Jesus' teachings. He admonished people to relate in loving and forgiving ways. If they did that conscientiously, they would become loving and forgiving people. Acting differently leads to feeling differently.

Teddy Roosevelt lived in the Badlands area for a couple of years after his first wife died. He wrote home once, saying that he was afraid of many things, such as gunfighters and grizzly bears. "But by acting as if I was not afraid, I found that I became unafraid." The psychiatrist Helmuth Kaiser once was swimming in the Mediterranean Sea, when he realized that the tide was pulling him out to sea. He looked around and saw a fishing boat nearby, to which he could have called for help. But he knew that if he did, he would become frightened—which he did not want to do. Fright would have increased his stress level and clouded his judgment. So he did what he had been taught—he swam parallel to the shore until he was out of the riptide.

Ultimately, forgiveness is based on tapping into a level of spirituality that is deeper than the level of the offense. Two understandings are especially relevant.

The first of these is the realization that in a profound sense, we create the world in which we live. We create our special world by the things we give importance to. By giving importance to something (or someone), it becomes real; it becomes part of our world. If we withhold importance, it loses its power over us.

The second understanding is that in a sense, we are all multiple personalities. We all enter into various mind-sets, or subpersonalities, several times a day. What I do in one mind-set does not express the totality of who I am. It is only a part of me. The same is true of one who offends me. He or she is not totally defined by the offense.

The next four chapters elaborate on these understandings.

Chapter 8

How I Create My Inner World

My world should be neither too large nor too small,
neither too demanding nor too indifferent.
It should be a world in which I can be
significant but not dominant,
limited but not overwhelmed,
helpful but not overly responsible,
loved but not worshipped.

Time heals all wounds.

Circumstantial evidence is a very tricky thing. . . . It may seem to point straight to one thing, but if you shift your own point of view a little, you may find it pointing in an equally uncompromising manner to something entirely different.

(Arthur Conan Doyle,
*Adventures of Sherlock Holmes:
The Boscombe Valley Mystery.*)

Many years ago, when I worked in a large state mental hospital, I was therapist for a suicidally depressed young woman, Helen. A couple of months after she was discharged, she wrote me a most discouraging letter, telling me how depressed she was.

I thought a lot about how to answer her. If I commented on the depression, I would be emphasizing it. I would be telling her that it was the depression that was important, and I would therefore be reinforcing it. But there was more to her letter than just the depression. She expressed herself very clearly—something she could not have done prior to her hospitalization. So in my response, I acknowledged the depression, but commented at length about how clearly she was able to express herself. I gave reality and importance to her communicating, not just to what she was communicating about.

Helen wrote me back, thanking me for my letter, and saying how much better it made her feel. Some time after that, she sent me a poem:

I am a mason,
building my self
out of what happens to me
by choosing, shaping, arranging events.
And when I review
what I have made,
if I decide
I'm dissatisfied,
I'll start again,
choosing, shaping, arranging,
until I build the me
I want to be.

In a very real sense, we create the world in which we live—the personal world. We give importance to some things (people, events, characteristics, and so forth), and withhold importance from others. My personal world, then, consists of the things that are important to me. Those things are emotionally and spiritually real.

From this perspective, my ability to live well comes from knowing how to create my world skillfully. I want to give importance, reality, to things that enhance my well-being, and withhold importance from those that do not.

Some people seem unable to do this. They give importance to events and relationships that hurt or threaten them, that make them feel powerless.

I know that I often withdraw importance from people who do not value me. I don't take their criticisms seriously. I don't let them humiliate me. With people whom I value, and who value me, I take confrontation and criticism much more seriously because I know these people have my best interests at heart.

Forgiveness is based on the ability to withdraw importance from the offensiveness of an offense, and focus on how I will deal realistically with the situation and with the offender.

I don't want to say that it is easy to take importance away from something, or that we can do it by sheer willpower, but importance can be invested elsewhere. This happens with the passage of time. As I add to the richness of my life, the relative importance of an offense decreases and it is experienced in a different context. It will therefore have a different significance.

An analogy with photography is relevant. When I focus on an offense, it is like using a telephoto lens. I can examine the offense in exquisite detail and experience all its injustices and hurt. A wide-angle lens allows me to see the offense in the total context of my life. Instead of filling the frame, it is seen only as a small blotch in the total picture.

A survivor of the Nazi concentration camps said that those who survived were those whose world extended beyond the barbed wire fence. At a very deep level, they withdrew reality from the psychological impact of imprisonment, and gave reality to the broader world beyond. They gave importance to the riches of the inner realities of fantasy, memory, and hope.

Is this denial? Yes, in a sense. But not the kind of denial you and I are tempted to employ. The prisoners *could not* change anything in their external world. You and I usually have options about what we will or will not endure.

In a very moving passage, Dr. Viktor Frankl writes of how the memories and images of his wife sustained him.

> I heard her answering me, saw her smile, her frank and encouraging look. . . . her look was then more luminous than the sun which was beginning to rise. . . . I understood how a man who has nothing left in this world may still know bliss . . . in the contemplation of his beloved. In a position of utter desolation, when man cannot express himself in positive action, when his only achievement may consist in enduring his sufferings in . . . an honorable way—in such a position man can, through the contemplation of the image he carries of his beloved, achieve fulfillment. (Frankl, 1985, p. 57)

It is significant that Frankl, who emphasized the inner self, also emphasized forgiveness.

My friend Joe Cocke prepares exhibits at the Los Angeles Museum of Natural History. One day he took me, my son Rob, and my four-year-old grandson Ben to a room where a new exhibit was being prepared. Several full-size lifelike plastic heads were lying on the table. I glanced at Ben. He was looking at these heads with some alarm. His father noticed this also, and said cheerfully, "Look Ben, see the dollies? Aren't those nice dollies?" Ben seemed much relieved as he pointed to them and said, "Nice dollies!" He even waved good-bye to them when we left.

Rob had defined this aspect of Ben's world as friendly, familiar. This was a definition that Ben was delighted to accept.

A friend told me that when he was in college, he bent over backward to make top grades on the first test of each course. That defined him to the teacher as a good student. When he made lower grades later in the year, the teacher just thought that he was having a bad day.

I did something similar with my grandchildren. During my grandson Ashley's first months, I watched carefully for any change in his expression while his sisters were looking at him, and would exclaim excitedly, "Look, he's smiling! He likes you! He likes you!" I was trying to create a reality of affection between them.

A well-known experiment with schoolchildren is relevant. A teacher is told that she is very fortunate to have Jack Smith transferring to her class. He is an outstanding student, a high achiever, and will be a delight in the classroom. The teacher will then treat Jack like an outstanding student. Sure enough, Jack becomes an outstanding student. His IQ will actually rise!

Unfortunately, a teacher may "warn" another teacher that a new student is a problem child and a troublemaker. This might well be a self-fulfilling prophecy.

In a passage that has been terribly misunderstood, Jesus spoke of creating your own world in relation to someone else's aggression. "If someone strikes you on the right cheek, turn the other to him also."

Many people have taken this as an admonition to accept abuse, to let someone else exercise power over them. I see it as just the opposite. I see Jesus' words as encouraging us to take charge of our lives.

If I hit you, I am defining you as an enemy. If you hit me back, you are agreeing, "I am your enemy." You are letting me define you in relation to me. You are giving me power over you.

But if you turn the other cheek, you are saying, "Wait a minute. I'm not your enemy. I'm not your enemy." It is a way of taking control of your life. *You* are defining you, rather than letting me define you. You are exercising a deeper level of control—not over me, but within yourself.

Margaret was in a rotten mood. Things had not been going well for her for some months, and she was angry at the whole world for not treating her better. One day, her son stopped by for a short visit. She lit into him viciously. She accused him of abandoning her when he got married, of never tending to her needs and so forth. Billy just laughed and said, "Mom, I've felt that way lots of times. I never knew how to say it as eloquently as you did, but I've wanted to."

Billy was giving reality to their broader relationship, not just to the abrasiveness of the moment. Margaret said that her anger dissipated.

She had defined her son as an enemy. He did not accept that definition, but defined their relationship very differently. He turned the other cheek. She had defined their relationship as unequal: He had the power to nurture her, and was withholding it. By her accusation, she was assuming a dominant stance. He defined the two of them as equals, which is apparently what she deeply wanted all along.

This self-definition has an interesting facet. The ways I act tend to influence you to act in a similar way. If I treat you as a friend, you are likely to be friendly also. But if I treat you as an enemy, that tends to create enmity. If a husband and wife (or ex-spouses) are at terrible odds with each other, one may accuse the other of malice. That very accusation exacerbates whatever malice might have existed to begin with.

But you don't have to respond in kind. It is always possible for you to maintain your own world and not be drawn into mine. If you create a friendly world in relation to me, then I am the one who will experience the pull. Your goodwill will tend to draw me into your world.

A friend, Janet, met her daughter, Fran, for lunch. The daughter was wearing her hair in a way that reminded Janet of a wig. When she commented on that, Fran took serious offense and the atmosphere became very tense. Finally Janet asked Fran if they could start over. Fran agreed.

"Okay, I'm just now walking into the room to greet you. 'Fran, hi! I'm so glad to see you. You've got your hair done different! It looks very nice.'"

Fran responded warmly to this. Later, she took mother's hand and told her she was very grateful for what she had done.

So we can change our realities in many ways. We focus on different things in ourselves, and in the other person.

A friend, Bruce, is a recovering alcoholic. Once he told me he had been seriously depressed for the past few weeks. He had even spent the night with friends lest he be tempted to kill himself.

I reminded Bruce of his history. Two years ago, if he were depressed, he would simply have gotten drunk. That was a guaranteed short-term cure for depression, but that option was no longer viable for him. He was on a spiritual path of recovery that precluded getting drunk. But every spiritual path has its price. Sometimes that price is a period of depression. I thought his depression was a small price to pay for sobriety. By this way of thinking, I was offering Bruce a different reality.

A very different situation involved a man whose daughter had been killed by a drunk driver. Well into the grieving process, he began to remember her differently. He knew what she would say if she could visit him.

"I want you to remember me lovingly. Let those memories be a source of warmth and happiness—not a source of continual devastation. I want your life to be richer because of what we shared, not poorer because of what we no longer share. I'm grateful that we were part of each other's lives for a while. I want you to be grateful also. Let the memories of my love, my playfulness, my values enrich your life. You will honor me most by having a full and rich life."

Our world is also defined by what we do *not* attend to—what we withhold importance from.

In the early 1960s, the United States discovered that the Soviet Union was installing offensive missiles in Cuba. President Kennedy sent a strong message of protest to the Soviet dictator, Nikita Khrushchev. He told him that all Soviet ships to Cuba would be stopped and searched. If they were carrying missiles, they would be turned back.

Khrushchev's reply was belligerent, implying the threat of war. Kennedy and his staff studied this reply for some time, and finally decided not to respond to it—to withhold reality from it. The next day, they received a much more conciliatory message from Khrushchev, and the crisis abated.

I attended a psychotherapy conference many years ago. As part of the conference, some twenty of us met with a well-known group therapist for a four-hour session. At the beginning, somebody said something about herself, and then somebody else said something, and then somebody else. Then there were a few moments of silence. Finally a man with a Midwestern accent (a psychiatrist, I think) proclaimed pompously, as if a revelation from God, "It seems to me that you people are trying to get to know one another."

As you can imagine, our reaction was instant hostility. There was an undercurrent of grumbling, and three or four people made sarcastic or caustic comments. Then a therapist from Atlanta, Dr. John Warkentin, said warmly to this man, "I wonder if you would say some more, so we could hear your voice and get a sense of knowing you."

Suddenly the whole group was different. John had interpreted the man's comments as his wish to make contact with us, however awkwardly. The rest of us had reacted only to the haughtiness of his manner. John saw beyond that to his wish for contact. By his response, John gave reality to this underlying wish and withheld reality from the haughtiness.

Perhaps this wish to make contact underlies most of the things people say and do. If that is so, then we most honor people when we react to that dimension of their behavior, no matter how crude its expression.

I have an old phonograph record of the pianist Walter Gieseking playing the Grieg piano concerto, opus 16. The fidelity is bad and there is an underlying hissing noise along with several small scratches. But the performance is wonderful. Usually, I can tune out the imperfections and hear just the music.

I think of this when I remember my parents. They were good people, but they made mistakes in raising me and my sister. Some were from ignorance. Some had to do with their personalities. Some grew from pettiness, or their wish to have children they could show off. Many of their mistakes had to do with their relationship with each other, which was very poor. But underneath all that, I knew they had my best interests at heart, more so than anyone else I would ever know—more than spouse, friends, children, more than I myself sometimes.

If I focus on their deficiencies, I will be angry and resentful. But if I focus on their positive characteristics—as I hope my children will do with me—then I will not only forgive them, but will also be able to appreciate them.

I realize that not all people have been as fortunate as I, to have had parents who were basically loving. Their experiences will then be different. But all parents are a mixed bag, as were their parents before them, as are we, and as our children will be.

Psychiatrist Carl Whitaker once worked in a residential treatment center for disturbed kids. One of the patients was a twelve-year-old girl who had been introduced into prostitution by her mother four years earlier. Cathy was already hard and cynical about life, but was beginning to make some progress. She was relaxing her defensiveness and letting certain people see her vulnerability.

One day she and a friend were sitting at a table in the lounge when two other girls walked up and began viciously berating Cathy. Carl said he could see the fragile self-esteem drain from her soul. Finally the girls finished their denunciations and walked off. Cathy and her friend sat in silence for a few moments. Then the friend said cheerfully, "Hey Cathy, let's go get a Coke."

Carl said he was profoundly moved by this act of acceptance. The friend did not address the insults directly. That would have sounded phony. She didn't tell Cathy not to pay attention to them. That would have been impossible. Instead, she simply did not give reality to the insults. She said by her behavior, "You and I are friends. That is all that is important."

My friend Joel related an interesting incident to me. He had said something that offended his wife, and she criticized him rather harshly. The next day, she apologized.

He said it took him a moment to remember what she was referring to. He had not taken offense at her criticism and certainly did not regard it as something that needed an apology. He told her that he knew she loved him; her anger did not threaten that. She was not out to change the nature of their relationship; she was not out to dominate or humiliate him. Her criticism was *within* a loving, stable relationship. She was just commenting on some of the details.

He had given reality not to the critical part of her criticism, but to the broader reality of their love for each other.

The carpet mills in north Georgia discharge various toxins into the rivers. Abundant rainfall in the spring and summer makes the river flow high enough to dilute the toxins, and they do not damage the life of the river. In the fall and winter, however, the flow is greatly reduced. If the same level of toxins were discharged during these periods, they would kill all the life in the river. For Joel, the flow of love was high, and the toxins were easily dissipated.

One woman was raped at knifepoint in her home. She calmly endured the rape, devoting her energies to thinking about how to escape. When the man rolled over, she seized the moment and ran for the door and outside to a neighbor's house. When the police came, she calmly described the incident and what she could remember about the man.

One police officer said to her, "Lady, you have just been raped. How can you be so calm about this?"

She replied, "You don't think I'm going to let twenty minutes with that so-and-so ruin my life!"

I hope she was able to get beyond the offense that easily. She was obviously a mature woman with many strengths, not a sixteen-year-old girl. I think for most of us, such a trauma has serious repercussions. It usually takes time and some serious work toward recovery before we can step into this woman's attitude. But healing is based on her principle: "I am not going to let some so-and-so ruin my life."

If I were to forgive my friend Alexander, I would have to focus on and nurture the things that enrich my life. I would have to reconnect with people who value me and like me. I would need to enlarge my world, so that Alexander's betrayal was seen from a different stance and in a different context.

I would like to close this chapter with an exercise. Think of someone who needs your forgiveness, someone who is important to you. This person has offended you seriously enough that a breach has occurred in your relationship. The person knows that he or she has offended you. Perhaps one or both of you have tried to take steps toward healing, but for whatever reason, they were not effective.

Now in your imagination, create a scenario in which this person apologizes to you and makes restitution! Imagine what he or she would say. What would you say in return? How would inner healing result from this? Give some time and thought to this experiment.

Now plan to spend some time with that person *as if* you had for-given him or her. Act as you would act if the apology and restitution had taken place. Create this reality for yourself. You will not bring up the offense(s); you will focus on things that represent other aspects of your relationship. You will affirm other realities of your lives. In this way, you are creating your world differently.

The remarkable thing is that if you treat the other as though you had forgiven, he or she will tend to act as though he or she had apolo-gized, and will be drawn into that new reality that you have created.

Chapter 9

One Example: Terry Dobson's Story

A soft answer turneth away wrath.

Proverbs (15:1)

Some people have a remarkable ability to create their own realities. Terry Dobson has described one such person. He writes:

A turning point in my life came one day on a train in the suburbs of Tokyo in the middle of a drowsy spring afternoon. The old car clanking and rattling over the rails was comparatively empty—a few housewives with their kids in tow, some old folks out shopping, a couple of off-duty bartenders studying the racing form. I gazed absently at the drab houses and dusty hedgerows.

At one station the doors opened and suddenly the quiet afternoon was shattered by a man bellowing at the top of his lungs, yelling violent, obscene, incomprehensible curses. Just as the doors closed, the man, still yelling, staggered into our car. He was big, drunk, and dirty, dressed in laborer's clothing. His bulging eyes were demonic, neon red. His hair was crusted with filth. Screaming, he swung at the first person he saw, a woman holding a baby. The blow glanced off her shoulder, sending her sprawling into the laps of an elderly couple. It was a miracle that the baby was unharmed.

The terrified couple jumped up and scrambled toward the other end of the car. The laborer aimed a kick at the retreating back of the old lady, but he missed and she scuttled to safety. This so enraged the drunk that he grabbed the metal pole in the center of the car and tried to wrench it out of its stanchion. I could see that one of his hands was cut and bleeding. The train lurched ahead, the passengers frozen with fear.

I stood up. At the time, I was young, in pretty good shape, was six feet tall, and weighed 225 pounds. I'd been putting in a solid eight hours of Aikido training every day for the past three years and thought I was tough. The trouble was, my martial skill was untested in actual combat. As a student of Aikido, I was not allowed to fight.

My teacher, the founder of Aikido, taught us each morning that the art was devoted to peace. "Aikido," he said again and again, "is the art of reconciliation. Whoever has the mind to fight has broken his connection with the universe. If you try to dominate people, you are already defeated. We study how to resolve conflict, not how to start it."

I listened to his words. I wanted to quit fighting. I had even gone so far as to cross the street a few times to avoid the *chimpira,* the pinball punks who lounged around the train stations. They'd have been happy to test my martial ability. My forbearance exalted me. I felt both tough and holy. In my heart of hearts, however, I was dying to be a hero. I wanted a chance, an absolutely legitimate opportunity whereby I might save the innocent by destroying the guilty.

"This is it!" I said to myself as I got to my feet. "This slob, this animal, is drunk and mean and violent. People are in danger. If I don't do something fast, someone will probably get hurt."

Seeing me stand up, the drunk saw a chance to focus his rage. "Aha!" he roared. "A foreigner! You need a lesson in Japanese manners." He punched the metal pole once to give weight to his words.

Hanging on lightly to the commuter strap overhead, I gave him a slow look of disgust and dismissal—every bit of nastiness I could summon up. I planned to take this turkey apart, but he had to be the one to move first. And I wanted him mad, because the madder he got, the more certain my victory. I pursed my lips and blew him a sneering, insolent kiss that hit him like a slap in the face. "All right!" he hollered. "You're gonna get a lesson." He gathered himself for a rush at me. He would never know what hit him.

A split second before he moved, somebody else shouted. "Hey!" It was ear splitting. I remember being struck by the strangely joyous, lilting quality of it, as though you and a friend had been searching diligently for something, and had suddenly stumbled upon it. "Hey!"

I wheeled to my left, the drunk spun to his right. We both stared down at a little old Japanese man. He must have been well into his seventies. He took no notice of me but beamed delightedly at the laborer, as though he had a most important, most welcome secret to share.

"C'mere," the old man said in an easy vernacular, beckoning to the drunk. "C'mere and talk with me." He waved his hand lightly. The big man followed, as if on a string. He planted his feet belligerently in front of the old gentleman, towering threateningly over him. "Talk to you," he roared above the clanking wheels. "Why the hell should I talk to you?"

The old man continued to beam at the laborer. There was not a trace of fear or resentment about him. "What'cha been drinkin'?" he asked lightly, his eyes sparkling with interest.

"I been drinkin' sake," the laborer bellowed back, "and it's none of your goddam business!" Flecks of spittle spattered the old man.

"Oh, that's wonderful," the old man said with delight, "absolutely wonderful! You see, I love sake, too. Every night, me and my wife (she's seventy-six, you know), we warm up a little bottle of sake, and take it out into the garden, and we sit on the old wooden bench that my grandfather's first student made for him. We watch the sun go down, and we look to see how our tree is doing. My great-grandfather planted that tree, you know, and we worry about whether it will recover from those icestorms we had last winter. Persimmons do not do well after icestorms, although I must say that ours had done rather better than I expected, especially when you consider the poor quality of the soil. Still, it is most gratifying to watch when we take our sake and go out to enjoy the evening—even when it rains!" He looked up at the laborer, eyes twinkling, happy to share his delightful information.

As he struggled to follow the intricacies of the old man's conversation, the drunk's face began to soften. His fists slowly unclenched. "Yeah," he said when the old man finished. "I love sake too . . ." His voice trailed off.

"Yes," said the old man, smiling, "and I'm sure you have a wonderful wife."

"No," replied the laborer. "My wife died." He hung his head. Very gently, swaying with the motion of the train, the big man began to sob. "I don't got no wife. I don't got no home. I don't got no job. I don't got no money. I don't got nowhere to go." Tears rolled down his cheeks, and a spasm of pure despair rippled through his body. Above the baggage rack a four-color ad trumpeted the virtues of suburban luxury living.

Now it was my turn. Standing there in my well-scrubbed youthful innocence, my make-this-world-safe-for-democracy righteousness, I suddenly felt dirtier than the drunk was.

Just then the train arrived at my stop. The platform was packed, and the crowd surged into the car as soon as the doors opened. Maneuvering my way out, I heard the old man cluck sympathetically. "My, my," he said with undiminished delight. "That is a very difficult predicament, indeed. Sit down here and tell me about it."

I turned my head for one last look. The laborer was sprawled like a sack on the seat, his head in the old man's lap. The old man looked down at him, all compassion and delight, one hand softly stroking the filthy, matted head.

As the train pulled away, I sat down on a bench. What I had wanted to do with muscle and meanness had been accomplished with a few kind words. I had seen Aikido tried in combat, and the essence of it was love, as the founder had said. I would have to practice the art with an entirely different spirit. It would be a long time before I could speak about the resolution of conflict." (Dobson, 1982, pp. 128-132)

This is a beautiful and powerful example of how one creates one's reality. The old man by his tone of voice and his whole demeanor said to the laborer, "I am not your enemy. I am not a threat. I am not like the foreigner who is getting ready to challenge you." To underscore his nonthreatening stance, he did not even stand up.

He then achieved two excellent areas of agreement with the laborer, although I am sure that neither the old man nor the laborer were aware of this. First, the old man gave the laborer a suggestion. He said, "C'mere." By coming, the laborer took a step into the old man's world. This implied that he would be open to other invitations to enter that world; he would be receptive to other suggestions from the old man.

Implicit in the old man's invitation was the understanding that they would *talk* with each other. "C'mere and talk with me." Even Dobson did not realize that by moving toward the old man, the laborer had implicitly agreed to limit his sphere of activity. He came to *talk*.

The old man's words, "C'mere and talk with me," were an offer of friendship. *He completely ignored the laborer's insulting curses.* He did not give reality to them. If he had addressed these insults, the laborer would have had to pursue them—he certainly was in no mood to back down. But when the old man just ignored the insults, the laborer forgot about them. Their reality just faded away. The old man obviously did not base his self-esteem on how this other man treated him. He was therefore free.

He next found a point of contact with the man. They both loved sake. An enemy emphasizes differences between himself or herself and the other. The old man found a similarity. Most people would have implied that the laborer was wrong for drinking sake, but the old man told him that sake was wonderful. He then proceeded to describe circumstances in which sake can be wonderful.

An enemy withholds information, especially about himself or herself. The old man shared information about himself with the laborer. He told him about himself, his wife, his grandfather, his great-grandfather, his home, his garden, his evening ritual, and a tree about which he was worried. The world into which he was inviting the laborer was gentle and life affirming. The laborer may even have found some symbolic parallel between the tree and himself. Perhaps he too had suffered through many of the "ice storms" of life. Perhaps the quality of the "soil" in which he had lived was very poor.

Twice the old man used the phrase, "you know," implying that they shared a commom reality. They were like old friends conversing, not strangers in an adversarial stance.

When the laborer's voice softened, the old man implied there was another area of similarity. He asked him about his wife. He had previously withheld reality from the abusiveness; now he gave reality to the softening—he implied that the laborer was worthy of a wonderful wife. His comment may also have reminded the man of his loneliness and neediness. By bringing up this area, he was addressing the laborer's neediness lovingly.

If I am acting in a belligerent and obnoxious manner, but you find some way to interpret my behavior as benign, it is extremely difficult for me not to accept that, for me to contradict you. It is extremely difficult to maintain anger in the face of gentleness, to maintain aggression when faced with nondefensiveness.

The laborer accepted the old man's definition of him and the situation. He accepted the old man's creation of reality, and responded with gentleness and hope.

Chapter 10

The Many Facets of Who I Am

[T]o enjoy each other for what you are, and to forgive each other for what you are not.

From a contemporary wedding service

I have a friend whose father, Frank, was in middle management with a company that had been involved in a long and bitter labor dispute. Frank was a serious and thoughtful churchman. He really tried to make his faith relevant to his whole life—including his work.

Most of the members of the church he attended were members of the labor union, and Frank supported the strike at first. After some months, management finally took labor's grievances seriously and made some major changes that to Frank seemed fair and honorable. Labor, however, would not accept them. The strike went on and on, becoming progressively more mean and bitter, and finally destructive and violent.

It seemed to Frank that labor wanted to punish the company rather than work for constructive change. As a thoughtful, spiritual person, he could not in good conscience be part of that, so he went back to work.

As soon as he did, the union people in his church treated him with contempt and rejection. They would not work with him on a committee; they would not sit next to him in Sunday school class or in the worship service. They would not kneel next to him at the communion rail. He even recognized some of the church members in cars that parked in front of his home in the late afternoon, to harass him as he came home from work.

My friend said his father expected that kind of hostility from the community, but not from his church. He expected the church to be the one place where people's differences could be transcended, where healing and reconciliation took place. It felt to him as if these people's commitment to their cause took precedence over their commitment to God. Why couldn't two believers kneel together in prayer, and affirm that at least for a few moments, there was a unity deeper than all their differences? When he realized this was not the case, Frank became quite depressed for several months.

This kind of polarization is not uncommon in our culture. It is easy to think of another person in terms of *one* characteristic, and then treat him or her as though that one factor totally characterized the person. This certainly makes life simpler, but also much more shallow.

It doesn't have to be that way. Consider a letter from a Civil War Confederate soldier to his parents. He said something to the effect that in the evening, after the noise of battle had died down, the smoke had lifted, and the men had retired to their camps, it seemed the dead on both sides should rise up and the wounded should be healed. They would gather together around one campfire to sing familiar songs and laugh together as they told stories about their homes and their families.

In some of the European wars, there would sometimes be a truce on Christmas Day. Soldiers from both sides would gather together to pray and sing carols and affirm an underlying unity as human beings that was deeper and ultimately more important than the conflict.

The tendency to see people in one dimension is especially strong when we are stressed out. It takes less emotional energy to see people in simplistic terms. The characteristics can be either positive or negative. There are times when I may naively trust someone when I should not. At other times I may regard someone as an enemy when he or she is not.

Seeing only one dimension leads to the terrible polarizations that characterize our culture: white/black, labor/management, liberal/conservative, gay/straight, and on and on and on. We see only one facet of the other person or group, and therefore treat them with scorn and contempt. Racism, sexism, and the other isms reflect the tendency to see other people only in terms of one characteristic.

This is especially true when someone offends me, especially if the offense is serious. I tend to see him or her only in terms of the offense. He or she becomes one-dimensional for a while. A terrorist is a terrorist. Period. It would be extremely difficult for me to think of him or her as anything else.

The reality is that we are all very complex persons. In a sense, we are multiple personalities. Each of our many mind-sets has its own mood, its own feelings, its own priorities, its own realities.

I see it most clearly in myself when someone tries to pressure me to do something I don't want to do. I can feel myself becoming a different person. I become stubborn and unyielding. I no longer listen with the same receptiveness. I shut off warmth to that person for a while. I can feel my muscles tense up; I become uncommonly alert and cautious. I choose my words more carefully. I am sure there are even subtle changes in my expression and posture. I become a different "person" than the "person" I typically am (or at least different from the "person" that I *think* I am).

I usually know what is happening, and I may or may not try to change it. But I don't have much control over the first few moments of this shift.

When I am with young children, something different happens. I shift into my playful self. I can feel a different kind of sparkle in my eyes, and my tone of voice changes. I become more animated. My mind even has access to different memories and different ways of thinking.

I have many other "selves": reflective, problem-solving, assertive, angry, depressed, cheerful, comforting, romantic, and others. I step into one or another of these mind-sets in response to situations in the world around me, or in response to my own inner processes.

I am aware that I also have a petty side. People who know me well have seen this—much more than I wish. Those who are my friends have been able to see more than just the pettiness. They value me for those other qualities. They give reality to those other things rather than just dismiss me for the pettiness. They forgive me for that part of me.

This way of understanding does not mean that I am not responsible for everything I do. It means that I am not totally identified with any one aspect of my self.

Children who are raised in two different cultures provide a graphic example of these different selves. A friend who was raised in Atlanta married a Japanese graduate student and moved to Japan, where she raised her family. Her children's world consisted of the home, which was fully American, and the outside world, which was fully Japanese.

She sees the effect most clearly in her youngest son. He is one person when speaking English, and a very different person when speaking Japanese. He even holds his body differently. She can tell by looking at him which culture he is embodying. I would think that if he were driving down the street, absorbed in listening to a Japanese song, he would react differently to a rude driver than if he were listening to an American song.

Harvard psychiatrist Robert Jay Lifton interviewed a number of the German doctors who had served at Auschwitz. He wanted to understand how a doctor could be part of such inhumanity. These were not run-of-the-mill doctors but were members of the Nazi Party. They were thus predisposed to a certain kind of arrogance and tolerance for cruelty. They had two primary functions at the camp: to control typhus, and to determine which incoming prisoners went to the slave labor camp and which went directly to the gas chambers.

Dr. Lifton said there was something about the whole milieu at Auschwitz that accepted this kind of dehumanization as normal. It had its own worldview that pervaded everything. Within a matter of *hours,* a newcomer would be caught up in that mind-set and would become a different person. Only a very few were able to resist it.

Dr. Lifton described it as a kind of psychological splitting. When the doctor was at home with his family, he could be a loving, gentle person, but when he put on his uniform and entered his work station, he became a different person. He had different values, different feelings, a different worldview. He was not just playing a different role but actually became that role for a while (Lifton, 1988).

Even more extreme than this is the true multiple personality. The splitting is at such a deep level of the psyche that the various personalities have only a vague sense of one another. People who suffer from this disorder usually were seriously abused as children. They coped with the abuse by tuning out the self that was being abused, and retreating into a different self. So profound are these differences that a person may be allergic to cats in one personality but not in another.

As long as the offender is seen as one-dimensional, any thought of healing in the relationship is impossible.

A middle-aged doctor, a man who took his marriage very seriously, had a brief affair with a nurse during a period of deep depression. He confessed this to his wife, assured her it would never happen again, and asked for her forgiveness. She was furious. She *would not* forgive him. She said she could never again trust him, and could never again open herself to him. For over a year, she was cold and abrasive, despite his sincere efforts to make a new beginning.

Finally three things happened. Her husband stopped badgering her to forgive him. The issue of forgiveness had become a power struggle between them. If she forgave him, then he won! He found some way to step out of that conflict. Also, her pastor talked with her about her husband's neediness. He was not motivated primarily by malice or vanity, but by anxiety and depression. He was not the incarnation of evil.

The wife also came to understand some of the rich complexity of her own life. She saw that she too was imperfect, needy. Yes, she had been victimized, betrayed, but there was much more to her than just that. In many ways, she could take charge of her own world, her own reactions, her own meanings. With these new ways of looking at the situation, the two of them were able to rebuild their relationship.

From the perspective of this chapter, personal maturity is related to the kinds of mind-sets at our disposal, and the ease with which can shift from one mind-set to another. This gives flexibility in dealing with life's complexities. Maturity is also related to our ability to see the multidimensionality of other persons.

In this sense, personal therapy and growth have to do with expanding one's repertoire, which includes the facility for creating easy transitions. I don't want to get stuck in just one kind of mind-set, no matter what the situation. I want to be able to choose wisely how I will react to different situations.

Imagine a highly specialized television system. It has many different channels, each with its own kind of programming. There are channels for comedy, horror, drama, romance, sports, news, problem solving, and so forth. An appropriate button is pushed, and a particular kind of program appears on the set.

In a similar way, when someone pushes my buttons, I gain access to a particular kind of programming. Over a period of time, the richness of my life is thus played out, but at any one moment, I may seem one-dimensional.

We tend to think of our reactions as unalterable. Someone pushes our buttons, and we react in a particular way. It may not occur to us to think of other ways we might have reacted. It is easy to live as though our reactions are absolutely and unalterably fixed. But in this analogy, the television system has the capacity for adjustment. The buttons can be retuned, to play out other channels. Psychotherapy can often help with this, and we can do a lot on our own.

If someone offends me, that doesn't mean that I have to tune in my revenge channel. It is possible for me to retune my responses to my problem-solving channel, or my forgiveness channel, or maybe even my compassion channel.

Some of my channels are sometimes inactive, and need to have some buttons reconnected to them. Other channels might have too many buttons that go to them. I may find myself tuning in my resentment channel much more often than I like. Maybe some of those buttons can be retuned.

I have a friend who is easily intimidated and especially sensitive to insults. She works in an office full of brash, angry men, who insult people as a matter of course, probably without even realizing it. My friend lives in a constant state of apprehension. She is afraid one day she is just going to burst out crying at one of these insensitive insults.

I reflected with her once about this analogy, and how she could retune some of the buttons. Her "insult" button was certainly exposed, and when somebody pushed it, that triggered her anxiety and depression channels. I thought it would be better if she could retune the insult button so that it would go to a different channel—maybe her curiosity channel. The next time somebody insulted her, that would be an excellent time for her to be really curious about why in the world somebody would behave in such a bizarre manner.

She laughed. "It's not bizarre when somebody insults you."

"Of course it is. And it is much better to be curious about this bizarre behavior than to be intimidated by it."

I suggested she form a picture in her mind of how she might react if her curiosity channel got turned on instead of her intimidation channel. She might find herself wondering what in the world was going on with this man. Was his wife giving him a hard time, or his kids? Was he in trouble with the IRS? Was his ulcer acting up? What was going on with him to make him act so strangely?

Parents sometimes slip into one-dimensional responses to their children. A child misbehaves, and Mom may tune in her "I've been a bad mother" channel. When parents feel this way, they often pressure their kids to be better, so they can stop feeling like bad parents. Think of how much more interesting it would be if Mom would retune the "misbehaving child" button so that it went to the "problem-solving" channel rather than to the "I've been a bad mother" channel.

Internally, forgiveness is based in part on gaining access to parts of me that were not damaged by the offender. I am more than just a victim. As I get in touch with those other aspects of myself, I can let go of the resentment that the victim in me feels.

Externally, forgiveness involves seeing the offender as a complex person. There is more to him or her than just the offending characteristics.

At a luncheon recently, I sat at the same table with Alexander. I noticed another friend looking at him with warmth. I remembered a time when he supported me through some difficulties. I found myself laughing at a joke he told. There was more to him than just the betrayal. That was one truth about him, but not the whole truth.

As I applied these understandings to my own situation, I did not experience a sudden miraculous transformation, but it did help. When I find myself caught up in resentment now and then, it helps to remind myself of these other realities.

Chapter 11

One Example:
Simon Wiesenthal's Story

Forgiveness is addressed to those whom we cannot excuse.

Simon Wiesenthal was a prisoner of the Nazis during World War II. One day when he was working at an army hospital, a nurse took him to the room of a dying SS soldier. The young man said he had wanted to see a Jew to apologize to him.

He told Wiesenthal first about his early life. As a youngster, he had joined the Hitler Youth, and then as an adult joined the SS.

One day while on duty, he watched as a group of Jewish families was herded into a house, which was then set afire. He and the other soldiers were ordered to shoot anyone who tried to flee. One woman with a baby in her arms, their clothes aflame, jumped from a window. He (and others) followed their orders and shot the baby and mother.

The young soldier was tormented by what he had done. A few days later, he was fatally wounded in battle. As he lay dying in the hospital, he asked to see a Jew. He told Wiesenthal this story and asked for his forgiveness as a Jew on behalf of the Jews he had killed.

Wiesenthal listened thoughtfully but felt he had no right to offer forgiveness on behalf of someone else. He walked out of the room without saying anything. He found out the next day that the soldier had died during the night.

After the war, Wiesenthal went to see the soldier's mother, who thought of her dead son as a good boy. He told her no differently.

Some years after the war, Wiesenthal (1998) wrote of his encounter with the young soldier. He wondered if he had been right in not offering forgiveness. He included in his book a number of responses by various scholars to this question. Most of them agreed that he had no right to forgive this man on behalf of someone else.

I read this story over two years ago and have thought about it often. I think I can finally address the issue. To me, the question is not "Do I have the right to forgive on behalf of another?" The deeper question is "How can I validate someone's commitment to change?"

Opposing forces were struggling within this young soldier: light and darkness, good and evil, decency and brutality. During his growing-up years, the darkness that engulfed his country also engulfed him. The darkness prevailed when he shot a Jewish woman and her child.

However this soldier was more than just the darkness, the brutality. He also had humane and decent qualities. Even before he lay dying, this humane part began to surface and tormented him about what he had done. The light within him, the decency, began to prevail.

Then as he lay dying, he wanted to see a Jew in order to renounce the darkness. He authorized Wiesenthal to hear his confession and to authenticate the light. In a sense, he ordained him to serve as priest. He wanted his life finalized in the light, not the darkness.

What would I have done if I had been in Wiesenthal's place? If I had had two years to think of a response, I might have said something such as this:

> I do forgive you on behalf of all Jews. I acknowledge your repentance, your turning away from brutality. You are renouncing the darkness in you and affirming the light. The real you is the decent you. I want you to die in peace.

Since I would have had only two minutes to think of what to say, rather than two years, so I probably would have done as Wiesenthal did.

Is it possible to forgive on behalf of someone else? Can even God meaningfully forgive on behalf of another?

Jewish law indicates that sins against God can be absolved by simple repentance, but for sins against another human being to be absolved, restitution must occur. The sinner must first secure the forgiveness of the one offended. No one has the right or power to forgive on behalf of another.

This idea is in many ways very appealing. It emphasizes accountability and does not allow offenders to go their merry ways, blissfully indifferent to the suffering that has been inflicted. Serious offenses demand atonement.

I find this concept troubling. Should the Nazi doctors live forever in remorse? Their victims cannot forgive them. Neither can their relatives, if they believe as Wiesenthal did. Should the former Nazis never experience love and happiness? Should they never laugh? Or is there a forgiveness that might enable them to say, "I cannot undo the past. I cannot change the things I have done. What I can do is live to the best of my ability with integrity and humility."

An item in the news several years ago discussed a young woman who was raped and killed. At the trial, her father testified that he *knew* his daughter would offer her forgiveness to her killer. She would not want to be in the presence of God with resentment in her heart, but she would also want to make sure that other people were protected from this man. She would want him imprisoned for as long as he was dangerous.

PART V:
MAKING IT HAPPEN

You can receive your own future only by releasing others from their pasts.

Forgiveness occurs as I tap into levels of spirituality that are deeper than the levels of the offenses: I can forgive offenses against freedom as I find deeper levels of personal freedom. I can forgive offenses against self-esteem as I base my self-esteem on deeper realities. I can forgive offenses against intimacy as I affirm deeper levels of connectedness with other people, with my world, and with my God.

Many things can push us to these deeper levels of spirituality. None does that with quite the same urgency as the offenses and injustices we suffer. It is easy to flit around on the surfaces of life as long as everything is going smoothly, but when suffering occurs, it is not enough to stay on the surfaces. We are pushed to find deeper foundations for our lives.

From this perspective, some offenses can actually be welcomed. They push us to gain access to those deeper levels of spirituality. People whose lives are relatively free of offenses may never be pushed in the same way to cultivate this deeper self, the spiritual dimension of their lives.

Forgiving a serious offense can be thought of as a transition from one mind-set (or feeling or kind of relating) to another. This is what happens when one initiates forgiveness. Such transitions are often extremely difficult, and we look to something in the external world (such as an apology) to make the transition possible.

I remember an incident when my young daughter Linda had stubbed her toe and was crying. I picked her up gently and hugged her. After a few moments, the tone of her crying changed. It sounded like she didn't *need* to cry anymore, but she didn't know how to stop. So I commented on something unrelated to the crying—I think I asked her what game she and her friend had been playing. She responded excitedly, apparently grateful that I had made the transition easy.

Even a forced forgiveness can be an effective transition. When young children fight, an adult often intervenes. The adult declares the conflict over and tells the kids to shake hands. By implication, both kids are declared equal, and so they can drop the effort to dominate each other.

In troubled families, it sometimes takes a catastrophic event, such as serious illness or death, to facilitate a transition. Sometimes even that is not sufficient.

Chapter 12

Forgiving Offenses Against Freedom

Whatever does not kill me strengthens me.

Nietzsche

To forgive someone who has compromised my freedom, I must gain access to a deeper level of freedom. When confronted with one who has abused power over me, I must gain access to deeper levels of personal power.

No one has done this more persuasively than Viktor Frankl. In the Nazi concentration camps, people were not only enslaved but knew their chances of dying or being murdered were quite high. Survival seemed to depend in large part on psychological and spiritual factors rather than just on physical ones. Many prisoners survived horrible physical deprivations; others who were still relatively healthy succumbed very quickly.

Those who survived had an ability to keep the inner self from being enslaved. Some created elaborate fantasy lives in which they were free. Others directed their attention to the successes of the past or to dreams of the future. Their world extended beyond the fence.

Frankl wrote of one particularly terrible day when he found himself obsessed with the endless "little" problems of his miserable life. Suddenly,

> I became disgusted with the state of affairs which compelled me, daily and hourly, to think of only such trivial things. I forced my thoughts to turn to another subject. Suddenly I saw myself standing on the platform of a well-lit, warm and pleasant lecture room. In front of me sat an attentive audience on comfortable seats. I was giving a lecture on the psychology of the concentration camp! All that oppressed me at that moment became objec-

tive, seen and described from the remote viewpoint of science. By this method I succeeded somehow in rising above the situation, above the sufferings of the moment, and I observed them as if they were already of the past. Both I and my troubles became the object of an interesting psychoscientific study undertaken by myself. (Frankl, 1985, p. 94f)

The experiences of camp life show that man does have a choice of action. . . . We who lived in concentration camps can remember the men who walked through the huts comforting others, giving away their last piece of bread. They may have been few in number, but they offer sufficient proof that everything can be taken from a man but one thing; the last of the human freedoms—to choose one's attitude in any given set of circumstances, to choose one's own way. (p. 86)

During one brutally harsh winter, Dr. Frankl was asked to say something encouraging to his fellow prisoners. He did not know how to respond to this, since he felt as discouraged and hopeless as they, but since they had asked him, he could not refuse. He spoke of the things in the past that had given meaning to their lives—meanings that could never be taken from them. He spoke of the future and the importance of hope. He then spoke of the present and of the many opportunities to give meaning to their lives (Frankl, 1985).

Reflecting on his experiences, Frankl stated:

What was really needed was a fundamental change in our attitude toward life. We had to learn ourselves and, furthermore, we had to teach despairing men, that *it did not really matter what we expected from life, but rather what life expected from us.* We needed . . . to think of ourselves as those who were being questioned by life—daily and hourly. (Frankl, 1985, p. 98)

In this deeper sense, Frankl was free. No one had ultimate power over him.

A young woman, Patricia, was eight months pregnant with her first child. One morning her husband left early for work, while she slowly got out of bed. A few minutes later, she heard him come back, and wondered what he had forgotten. He came to the bedroom and sat down on the bed beside her to put his arms around her. He kissed her on the forehead and said that he had just come back to tell her again how much he loved her. On the way to work, he was hit by a drunk driver and killed.

At first, Patricia was devastated. After a while, that gave way to despair and hopelessness, then to rage. The rage soon came to consume much of her energy for living and caring for her child. The time came when she was ready to let go of the rage, to let this atrocity stop controlling her.

One of the ways she did this was to think of the accident as a tragedy rather than an offense that was directed against her personally. The drunk driver did not even know his victim, and was not even aware of what he had done.

Also, she kept asking herself how her husband would want her to handle the situation. Would he want this tragedy to dominate the rest of her life? Would she be more loyal to him by hating the killer forever, or would she be more loyal by having a good life, with laughter and love and purpose?

With these questions came a gradual release, a forgiveness, that enabled her to build a happy life. She took control of the meanings by which she lived.

Learning about these experiences put the betrayal by my friend Alexander in a very different frame of reference. I had not lost the ability to think or to feel. I had not lost the ability to connect with people who love me. I had not lost my freedom to choose my own priorities. I was still in charge of my life.

This ability was mine in reference to other situations also. Shortly after the incident with the rude driver, I told a friend about it and about my reactions. He suggested I pray that God would send me *more* rude drivers, so I could get more practice at forgiving.

That was not what I wanted to hear!

But believe it or not, it made a difference for me. When I am able to adapt my friend's suggestion to my own lifestyle, I end up feeling somewhat generous, moral, and a bit more in control of my own life in relation to rude drivers.

Rude drivers are often people who are angry and narcissistic much of the time. If I "get even" with them, such as by an obscene gesture or an angry blast of my horn, I will make them more angry. They are then likely to drive even more recklessly. So I can think of my "forgiving" as an act of public service. I will not make this lunatic driver even more dangerous.

As a therapist, I have had occasional clients who have described horrible persecutions by family, police, enemies, associates, aliens, and so forth. I do not think it is helpful to label these people as paranoid. They already feel traumatically out of control of their lives, and do not need to be afflicted with a demeaning diagnosis.

My job as a therapist is to help them find some areas they can control. One way to do this might be to suggest they pray for those who are persecuting them. This sometimes can take some of the edge off of the terror.

To forgive offenses against freedom, abuses of power, I tap into deeper levels of freedom and control.

Chapter 13

Forgiving Offenses Against Self-Esteem

Love your enemies and pray for those who persecute you.

Jesus (Matthew 5:44)

A young man who had recently joined a church consulted his pastor about the pervasive resentment he felt toward life. He was aware that he was disliked by both his peers and his employers because of his abrasive attitude toward everything. He wanted to be able to change that.

He told the pastor of an incident that occurred when he was in fourth grade that seemed to symbolize everything about his childhood. In the middle of the class period, he raised his hand for permission to go to the rest room. The teacher shook her head. He raised his hand again, urgently. Still no permission. Finally he could control himself no longer and wet his pants.

The teacher was irate at this. She seized him by the shoulders and dragged him to the front of the class, urine dripping from his pants, and made him write on the blackboard, "I will not pee in my pants in this class."

As he told his pastor of this incident, the shame of that humiliation flooded back. He buried his face in his hands and sobbed.

The pastor got up, walked around behind him, and put his hands on his shoulders. He asked him to imagine Jesus walking into that fourth grade classroom. He would put his arm around the student's shoulder and turn to the teacher. "Teacher," he would say, "this is no way to treat a boy."

Jesus, with his arm still around the boy, would then walk with him toward the door, leaving behind the teacher who had been mean to him, leaving behind the other kids who were nervously giggling, wondering if they would be the next ones to be humiliated by this teacher, leaving behind the unfinished sentence on the blackboard, leaving behind the little puddle of urine on the floor, and leaving behind once and for all time the shame and humiliation of that experience.

This simple intervention was a turning point for the young man. He became a different person and was eventually accepted as a valued member of his community.

There are several ways to understand what happened in that therapeutic moment. I want to mention only one. This fourth grade student had been humiliated by his teacher. She had abused her power over him. She had abused her role of teacher and her importance to him. She had damaged his self-esteem. That moment seemed to symbolize the many other humiliations he had suffered throughout his growing-up years.

The pastor drew on the young man's spiritual orientation, asking him to imagine Jesus comforting and defending him—valuing him. In so doing, he invited the young man to recognize and affirm a deeper source of self-esteem.

During the early days of the Civil Rights movement, one little black girl started first grade in 1960 in a previously all-white school. Much protest occurred, along with a complete boycott by the white community. She was the only child in the entire school.

Dr. Robert Coles, now a well-known child psychiatrist, came to New Orleans to observe how this little girl would handle the abuse to which she would be subjected.

At 2:30 that first afternoon, little Ruby walked out of the school, escorted by federal marshals. A crowd of angry people greeted her with clenched fists, threats, and curses. Day after day, this was her ordeal on entering and leaving school. The crowd tried deliberately to humiliate her.

According to the prevailing theories of childhood development, Ruby should had had severe psychological symptoms, but Dr. Coles could find none. She was eating well, sleeping well, cheerful, agreeable, happy. How could this be? Was she repressing her anxiety? Would it emerge later, in the form of neurosis? How could she take such abuse without being damaged?

Once on her way into school, Ruby stopped and appeared to be talking to someone in the crowd. When her teacher asked her about it, she said she wasn't talking with anyone. She said she had stopped and seemed to be saying something. She replied that she was stopping to pray for these people.

"To pray for them?"

"Yes. Don't you think they need to be prayed for?"

"What do you say when you pray for them?"

"I say, 'Father, forgive them, because they don't know what they are doing.'" (Bridges, 2000)

Dr. Coles later found out that she prayed for these people every night. The minister at her church prayed for them every Sunday. Ruby suffered no damage from the abuse. Her self-esteem came from within herself and from her family and community. She was in control of her attitudes! (I first heard this story many years ago. Several years later, I heard a slightly different version in a sermon. Then in 1998, a Disney television movie told Ruby's story.)

The offenses against self-esteem that most of us face are minor, such as insults. These can be extremely irritating if we have not developed a thick skin.

A thick skin is especially important in relation to children. Parents often make the mistake of wanting their children to be obedient—which is not only absurd but also perverse. Most of us have grown up with at least some sense that this is an appropriate concern.

If we have strong personal needs to be in control, it will be especially tempting to focus these needs on our children. We *will* make them obey, and of course all kinds of rationalizations are at our disposal to justify this. Some of the rationalizations are even religious. The passion to have obedient children leads to an approach to parenting that is based on power.

One mother said that her eight-year-old son could absolutely infuriate her with his defiant smirk when he would say, "You can't make me!" This is an invitation to a power struggle that no one can really win. When mother did succeed in *making* her son obey, it was terrible. The boy was humiliated and the mother was full of shame at what she had done.

A much happier approach is to ask for your children's cooperation rather than their obedience. Let their objectionable behavior be a challenge to your ingenuity rather than to your self-esteem.

If my son insulted me, for instance, or challenged my authority, I wouldn't want to put him down for that, or assert my authority. Such a response would come from an adversarial model of parenting. I would want to address him with nonchalance and forgiveness. I would want to have a thick skin. Trying to make children be obedient is not only a guaranteed recipe for power struggles, it is a violation of the deeper meanings of parenthood. I do not want to base my self-esteem on my children's obedience.

One mother told her rebellious child, "Of course I can't make you do something. I wouldn't want to. But what I can do is give you a hug and a kiss. Maybe later, we can sit on the couch together and I can read you a story."

Robert Coles (1997) tells of an infant who started throwing his bottle on the floor when he had finished feeding. His mother regarded this behavior as unacceptable, but was not going to get angry or punish her child. She made sure she was with her son when he finished feeding, and took the bottle from his hand *before* he could throw it on the floor. Within a short time, the child stopped playing this "game."

I remember a well-educated young man, Mark, whose memories of childhood were primarily of his father's criticism. I told him that men whose status needs are high often criticize. Looking for what is wrong with other people is one way to feel superior (high status). I then suggested that Mark think of his father's criticism as a kind of language (Mark speaks six different languages).

There are two ways to learn a language. You can be exposed to it over a long period of time, which is the way we learn our native language, or you can take lessons. Dad apparently was never exposed to the language of appreciation and never had the opportunity to take lessons. So he spoke the only language he knew—the language of criticism.

Mark was now learning the language of appreciation. As he spoke that language with his father, he felt he was forgiving him.

I tried to apply all these principles to my own situation in relation to the friend who had demeaned me by his betrayal. I could not change him. I could not *make* him value me, but I have other friends who do appreciate me. I also have my own inner self, where I experience God. I think these realities were crucial in my being able to forgive the one who betrayed me.

Chapter 14

Forgiving Offenses Against Intimacy

Love is the only power that can overcome evil without using evil means.

John Mogabgab

At one level, Alexander's betrayal was an offense against freedom. He limited some of my choices. It was relatively easy for me to forgive him for that. At another level, it was an offense against my self-esteem. He had used me, implying that I was unworthy of being treated decently. This also was relatively easy to forgive. At a deeper level, however, he had offended against my sense of intimacy. He had violated my trust and betrayed me. That hurt the most and was the hardest of all to forgive.

Our intimate relationships give us our deepest sense of identity and security. It is there that we find the affirmations and personal resources that enable us to forgive other offenses. It is there that we find the deepest meanings for our lives. Offenses against intimacy therefore undermine the sources of the things that enable us to forgive.

Most of the offenses against intimacy are committed by loved ones. This can make forgiveness quite complex.

There is a difference between forgiving an act and forgiving a person. To forgive an act, I minimize its importance. To forgive a person is just the opposite: I emphasize your importance. You are more important than what you have done; you are more important than your actions. So I forgive what you have done on the basis of who you are and what our relationship is. In so doing, I would hope to come to a deeper understanding of you, of me, and of our relationship.

How can one forgive offenses against intimacy?

A first step might be to ask myself what the consequences are of not forgiving. A loved one will die someday. If I have not forgiven that person, I will be left with much that is unresolved. Feelings such as anger, resentment, and alienation become more complicated after the offender is dead. The passage of time might soften the resentment, as it creates a broader context in which to put offenses. But I am much more in control of things if forgiveness comes from my own choice and initiative rather than from the mere passage of time.

It helps to understand that the loved ones who are so hard to forgive are merely ordinary fallible human beings, like the rest of us. Personality aspects that hurt us—stupidity, pettiness, pride, or even malice—do not represent the whole person. Forgiving them does not necessarily require reconciliation with them, but it does open the door to that possibility. To be able to see more than just the pathology can be immensely freeing.

It also helps to become aware of my own imperfections. If I can remember that I am not exactly perfect myself, that will make me aware of the kind of evenness that forgiveness seeks. To be unforgiving is to take a dominant stance over those who have hurt me. A loving relationship is based on a sense of equality, not dominance. I want to be loved, not pitied or appeased.

Many friends and loved ones have forgiven me for my offenses. I have often been forgiven even though I did not apologize or make restitution. I have been forgiven many times simply because others have been forgiving persons.

Perhaps this is part of what Jesus had in mind when he suggested that it was not appropriate to judge another, "for with the judgment you pronounce you will be judged" (Matthew 7:12). Or again, "take the log out of your own eye, and then you will see clearly to take the speck out of your brother's eye" (Matthew 7:5).

But does this imply that forgiveness is based more on our sickness than on our health? Must we always remind ourselves of our shortcomings? Isn't forgiveness stronger when based on our goodness rather than on our faults, on our generosity rather than on our poverty?

People who have forgiven me have seen more to me than just my weaknesses, my humanness. They have given importance, reality, to those other qualities. Reaching into my experiences of being forgiven may make it easier for me to forgive.

An offense against intimacy damages my sense of being connected to other people, therefore I need to reconnect by spending time with people who do love me and reaffirming my relationships with them.

Ultimately, the deepest sources of forgiveness for offenses against intimacy are similar to the sources of forgiveness for other offenses: I tap into a deeper level of spirituality. I gain access to a spirituality that is deeper and stronger than the offenses. I gain access to a spirituality in which my life is based not on being right, or being justified, or being a victim, but is based on deeper realities.

Arthur, who was approaching retirement, had owned several sailboats throughout his adult years. He belonged to a sailing club, as did a great many of his friends. His dream was to own a marina that would put him in daily contact with people who loved to sail.

When a suitable piece of land on the local lake became available, Arthur retired early and invested most of his savings in the pursuit of his dream. He asked his younger brother, whom he had supported emotionally and financially during a divorce, to go into business with him. Arthur would provide the capital and the overall planning; the younger brother would handle the day-to-day operations.

After two years, business seemed good, but there were no profits. Finally Arthur had the books audited and discovered that his younger brother had stolen approximately $80,000. When confronted with this theft, the younger brother fled the country.

Arthur's first reaction was helpless rage. How could his own brother do this to him? How could anybody betray his loving trust? He angrily stomped around the office for a half hour or so, yelling and cursing. Finally he realized that he was hurting himself by his behavior, and needed to address the situation in a different way.

He paused to take stock of his options, and remembered some advice a friend had given him years ago: turn it over to God. He closed his eyes for a moment and then got on his knees to pray. As soon as he knelt, he began to sob. Waves of sadness swept through him. The rage was gone, and he was in touch with a deeper and more authentic reaction: grief. He remembered the words of a well-known hymn: "let goods and kindred go . . ." which he repeated several times.

When he rose, he said he felt a strange peace within himself. He would try to track his brother down and recover what he could, but the intensity of his feeling had abated and it was now objective, not an inner devastation. He had reexperienced his connectedness with God, and thereby with all of life.

Many times, we must first mourn what (or whom) we have lost. Only then can we forgive.

It is useful for me to think of two sets of parents. One set of parents is external. They live (or lived) in certain places, did certain things, and have had a relationship with me that changed over the years. They are (or were) a mixed bag, like every other human being, with assets and liabilities, strengths and weaknesses.

The other set of parents lives within my psyche. These internal parents are reflections of the real parents I had when I was a child, but they are distorted. When I internalize, I inevitably exaggerate some characteristics and minimize others. Often, I will exaggerate the negative and minimize the positive. It is the internalized parents that are the most difficult to deal with, to forgive. When one has dealt with the internalized parents, it is much easier to deal with the external ones. This is one of the primary functions of psychotherapy.

If parents live long enough, they will get their act together someday. They will realize the stupid and destructive things they have done. But if they die or become senile before that happens, they lose the opportunity to make peace with their children. In that situation, you can only imagine what they would have said to you when they fully realized the kind of parents they had been.

I wrote earlier about Martha, whose husband had had an affair with her best friend. Martha explained that above all, she needed time to recover from the hurt. A part of her wanted Alan to hurt as much as she had, but she didn't know how to bring that about. It wasn't a matter of getting even. She needed him to understand how deeply his betrayal had hurt her.

Alan apologized to Martha as best he could, but his words carried little weight. Nothing he said seemed to make any difference—his sorrow, his promises, his efforts to atone for his betrayal. From Martha's perspective, he spoke from a position of strength, not pain. He was "supposed" to apologize and take steps to undo the wrong. She was then "supposed" to forgive him and put this behind them.

If Martha accepted his apology, as he wanted her to, would she be implying that he had not hurt her? Would she be giving him power over her again, letting him tell her what to do? Would he again be the one defining their relationship?

Martha was concerned that Alan did not take the affair seriously. She needed his assurance that he really understood how destructive it had been to her, and that kind of assurance cannot be conveyed in words. As time passed, she felt herself keeping a constant pressure on him, hoping he would understand how she felt.

Fortunately, Alan had the good sense not to refer to any of the extenuating circumstances. Had he done this, he would have been *demanding* her forgiveness—something that would make any real forgiveness impossible.

The affair had occurred during a period of high stress for him. In several important areas of his life, he faced situations that left him feeling inadequate and unloved. Martha had been absorbed in her own concerns at a time when Alan needed her comfort and nurture. She had been impatient and critical when he needed her support, so in a way, she had contributed to his neediness.

If Alan had pointed that out, it would have made things worse. He would have been minimizing his own responsibility. It would have implied that in similar circumstances, he might have another affair. If Martha had accepted this logic—that she had contributed to the things that motivated the affair—she would have been forgiving him from a position of weakness, not a position of strength. The betrayal left her feeling weak enough; she did not need that weakness reinforced.

Neither of them wanted to turn their conversations into a debate in which points were awarded for the most persuasive argument.

Martha had read once about a man who was lost in Death Valley, without water. Finally he came to a salt spring. He knew the water would poison him, but his thirst was so overwhelming that he could not refrain from drinking. Martha said this story helped her understand Alan. She could see the part of him that was immature and needy, rather than malicious. He was like a little boy, needing constant reassurance. It was only as she realized Alan's neediness that she began to realize how her own behavior had reinforced that neediness and contributed to the affair.

Martha had to look deep within herself—beyond healing and understanding—to forgive. She thought of other people with whom she had ties. Some of them were deeply loving and supportive; others were more casual. But all of them were important.

She also thought of her personal investments of time and energy in in music, church, hobbies, profession, home. In some ways, these had some of the same qualities of intimacy as did her relationships with people. She thought of her relationship with the world of nature and with God, both of which felt intimate to her. All of these spoke of her connectedness with life.

Martha came to realize that her capacity for intimacy was unchanged. Her connectedness with life was basically intact. No matter how other people behaved, she felt an undergirding sense of intimacy at the core of her life that became the base of her ability to forgive.

PART VI:
CONCLUSIONS

Focussing on the past brings resentment; focussing on the future brings anxiety; only by living in the present is there joy.

> Adapted from a well-known saying
> by Fritz Perls

Becoming a forgiving person doesn't just happen. It is part of a spiritual discipline. That discipline is composed of many parts—physical, mental, relational, emotional, and so forth. It comes from inner healing and growth; it is also a by-product of one's conscious choices. This book has emphasized the latter: you can make deliberate commitments that will help bring healing and growth to your inner self.

Becoming a forgiving person is part of your overall well-being. The things you do in each area of your life will affect the other areas.The following paragraph may seem out of place in a book on human relationships. I include it with the hope that you will take it seriously.

Your physical health is a very basic factor in your well-being. If you do not attend to your physical health, it will be more difficult to become a forgiving person. A healthy diet, rest, and exercise are important ingredients in your ability to forgive another person and to forgive yourself.

Finding an appropriate balance between work, play, and family is also important. I have spoken with a number of people who have retired or who are approaching retirement. As they reflected on their lives, many said they truly regretted the time and energy they invested in their work, and wished they had given more to their families. I have never heard anyone say he or she regretted the time and energy given to family, or wished more had been given to work.

A network of loving relationships—people who both affirm you and challenge you—is also important to your well-being. This too will help you forgive other people and yourself.

You can also stop subjecting yourself to TV and movies that portray intimidation and revenge as appropriate ways to live. These presentations have a considerable power to shape worldviews. When you do see dramas and reflect on the situations they portray, you might try to imagine how the drama would have unfolded if the protagonists had been forgiving persons.

If will be much easier to become a forgiving person if you have made peace with people whom you have hurt or alienated. Ask their forgiveness where that is needed. Specific persons may come to mind, along with specific steps that you can take to bring healing to that relationship.

Finally, the best way to become a forgiving person is to practice forgiveness. It may not come easily; it may be an imperfect forgiveness, but the deliberate decisions you make about how you act will help to shape your inner self.

Chapter 15

Pulling It All Together

The longest journey begins with a single step.

Chinese proverb

Here is how, hypothetically, some of the principles of forgiveness might be put into practice.

The need to forgive was brought home to Paul forcibly when his parents visited from out of state. He was aware of a lingering resentment for their inadequacies as parents—especially his father. Nothing was said, but when they left, he reflected on their visit.

Both parents were now in their seventies and in rather poor health. They would not be alive many more years. He imagined himself visiting their graves a year or so after their deaths. As he pictured this in his mind, he began to weep. He really wanted to be at peace with himself in relation to them. He wanted to tell them that he loved them— a sentiment that had always been blocked by his resentment. If he were to find that peace, he would have to do something soon.

He recalled some of their positive characteristics. There were many. He realized he could focus on these as well as on the negatives. He could create his world differently.

He then thought about himself in relation to his own children. He too had made many mistakes as a father, but he wanted his children to focus on his love for them—however imperfectly it was expressed. He now wanted to do this with his own parents.

He thought about his life. He had the freedom to make choices about his attitudes. His respect for himself came from within, not from without. There were people whom he loved and who loved him. In some way, it seemed that forgiveness would be based on these deeper levels of spirituality.

About this time, he read of a guided meditation that seemed very relevant. The next evening, when his family was out, he set aside a half hour for this exercise. He found a comfortable chair, closed his eyes, and let his thoughts focus inwardly. He remembered a mountain he had once climbed, and the sensation that he was in a sacred presence. Some of those feelings returned to him as he remembered.

After a few moments, he shifted his attention. He focused on his resentment toward his parents. He tried to remember specific offenses, and as he did so, he again felt negativity and resentment.

Then he shifted his attention back to the memory of the mountain, and the feelings this evoked in him. As he looked out on the world of plains and rivers and other mountains, he experienced power and goodness.

Then he returned to his resentment of his parents. He simply put himself in their presence, without any conscious thoughts or intentions.

He revisited the mountain. He imagined again what might transpire if he were really there. What qualities might be given to him that he could incorporate into the deepest levels of his psyche? How would the meanings of that experience express themselves in his life?

As he continued to meditate, he brought his parents into the scene on top of the mountain. He showed them the things that had been so meaningful to him. He slowly realized that he was forgiving them.

Another hypothetical person, Emma, took another approach. She asked a trusted friend to help her. She remembered that in Alcoholics Anonymous (in which she participated), psychotherapy, the church, and other spiritual traditions, confession is best done in the presence of another person. Why should this not be true for forgiveness also?

She told her friend that she was practicing a spiritual discipline, and wanted her as a friend to spend some time with her. She would ask only for her silent presence.

They met in a quiet place where they would not be interrupted, and sat facing each other, holding hands firmly. Emma looked at her friend and said, "I have reached an impasse at an important point in my life. I want your support as I think about it seriously. Please don't ask me what it is about. Just be with me while I look inwardly for healing and resolution."

Then she thought about the future and wondered, how will my relationship with Tom change after I have forgiven him? How might we relate to each other the next time we meet? How will my feelings be different? How might he be different?

Emma might not have realized it consciously, but to fantasize about the future is one step in creating that future, and it tends to draw one into it.

When Emma felt finished, she squeezed her friend's hand and thanked her. She told her friend she might never discuss with her what this was all about. For the present, she needed to keep all her energy for the task at hand.

You can put into practice one of the central teachings of Jesus: "Love your enemies, and pray for those who persecute you."

The most meaningful prayers are not verbal. In a visual prayer, you simply visualize the person in some situation. You may visualize him or her in the presence of God or in the presence of that which you regard as sacred, and let that scene unfold of its own accord. Or you may just hold the person in God's light without any activity. In this way, you are sending some of your own emotional energy out into the spiritual world. It may not bear fruit for the other person, but it will bear fruit for you.

A friend's mother, Elizabeth, was the youngest child in her family, with three older brothers. All of her cousins were male. As the only girl in the extended family, she had been adored and doted on as a child by the entire family. When Elizabeth reached adulthood, she expected this adulation to continue, and was incredibly sensitive to slights or—God forbid—insults.

Nobody in the family could remember the incident that led to her outrage against the family. They just knew it involved her older brother. Probably he did not give her the attention she thought she deserved. When she complained to the rest of the family about this brother, they told her she was overreacting. That led to her alienation from them as well. As with other family conflicts, this one escalated, with everyone eventually contributing to the discord.

The only person who supported Elizabeth was her daughter. Clara did not agree with her mother, but saw how fragile she was and did not want to make things worse.

Elizabeth owned shares of stock in a small company. When that company was bought out by a large corporation, Elizabeth suddenly had a large sum of money. She decided to give part of this money to Clara in appreciation for her support through the years.

Clara had seen a therapist for several years, and experienced a lot of personal reflection and growth. She was no longer intimidated by her mother's resentments.

When her mother offered to pay off the mortgage on her house, Clara told her she would accept the gift on one condition. She wanted to hear her mother say that she forgave everyone in the family for everything they had ever done to her. She also wanted to hear her say that she forgave herself.

Elizabeth was adamant in her refusal, but Clara insisted, gently but firmly. Elizabeth's younger son, who was there and to whom Elizabeth was still civil, told her that she could always retract her declaration.

Finally Elizabeth said the words—reluctantly. She said she forgave everyone in the family for the hurts they had inflicted on her. She forgave herself for her part in the conflict.

Maybe she wasn't totally sincere. Maybe she did have in mind the possibility of recanting. Nevertheless, she became a different person, and as she did, the hostility in the family gradually dissipated.

Saying the words committed her to living them. The words, even though they were tentative and imperfect, created and defined a different kind of future for her. That future then drew her into itself.

Close your eyes and imagine yourself in the presence of God. Say to God (or whatever symbolizes the sacred for you), "I forgive everyone who has ever hurt me, especially [name the person]. I also forgive myself for my part in the conflicts."

Chapter 16

Is Reconciliation Necessary?

So if you are offering your gift at the altar, and there remember that your brother has something against you, leave your gift there before the altar and go; first be reconciled to your brother, and then come and offer your gift.

Jesus (Matthew 5:23f)

It is better to be unhappy single than to be unhappy married.

A woman, Charlene, told of her father, who had deserted the family when she was three. Her mother was financially and emotionally unable to cope with the responsibility of raising three children, so the two eldest daughters went to live with grandparents while Charlene stayed with her mother, who was usually exhausted, irritable, and emotionally unavailable.

With Charlene's family suddenly gone, she began to create a new family—one that was more stable and reliable. She began a collection of stuffed animals. Throughout adolescence and into adulthood, these animals were immensely important to her. In a very real sense, they had become her companions, her consolation, her nurturers.

Charlene married in her early twenties. Unfortunately, her husband was intensely possessive and jealous. One day, she did something that offended him. When she got home from work the next day, she found all her animals laid out on the bed—with their bellies slit open.

Terrified by the obvious symbolism of this act and overwhelmed by the immensity of her loss, Charlene ran to a neighbor's home and retreated into an almost psychotic state of withdrawal. After several hours, her husband became worried about her and apologized for what he had done. He said he would buy her some more animals. Couldn't they just forget about what had happened?

Charlene was torn between conflicting wishes. She still suffered from a deep sense of insecurity. Even though the marriage was troubled, Kenneth did offer at least the appearance of security. On the other hand, she doubted very seriously that he could change—even if he wanted to, and he had given no indication that he really wanted to change.

When she hesitated to return home, he said, "Don't you trust me?"

I am all in favor of Charlene forgiving him inwardly, letting go of resentment and getting on with her life. *But to forgive does not mean to become stupid.* If Kenneth has abused her once, he will almost certainly abuse her again. In that sense, I think all persons are trustworthy. You can trust people to keep on being the way they have been.

If a man tells his wife, "I will never hit you again!" she can trust him to say those exact words again the next time he hits her. It is true that a person may change, but you can't depend on it. What you can depend on, what you can trust—and what you need to base your decisions on—is that unless he takes his character flaws very seriously, he will stay the same.

As Charlene reflected on the situation some months later, she said she now realized that to go back with Kenneth would have been suicidal. It might be her belly that was slit open next. She might be able to forgive him someday, but she wanted to make sure she never forgot.

After several years of struggle and two small children, Anne finally divorced Walter. Even though she realized the marriage was destructive to her, it gave her a sense of structure and purpose for her life. After the divorce, she was quite depressed for several months and buried herself in her work.

Walter was seriously narcissistic, irate at the thought that anyone would not think he was wonderful. He resented Anne deeply for the insult of leaving him, and consistently treated her with contemptuous disdain. He told the children that everything was Anne's fault: she was the one who wanted the divorce, her greed had impoverished him, she wouldn't let the kids visit when he could see them, and more.

Symptomatic of his contempt is the fact that he didn't write letters to her; he sent memoranda. For example:

Memorandum:
To: A. Thompson
From: Walter Zilch, PhD [he is a therapist, no less]
Subject: Visitation of children in July.

Anne said that this kind of depersonalization was the most painful thing about the divorce. After all, she was still the mother of his children.

For a long time, Anne tried to be placating, doing everything she could to salve his ego. His contempt continued, and she felt abused. She then tried to distance herself, having as little to do with him as possible. However, she could not do that without causing the children a lot of pain. Then she tried being straightforward about her anger, letting Walter know that she resented the ways he was treating her and the children. That made things worse. Finally, Anne entered therapy.

Her therapist, Lynn, knew that dealing with the ex-spouse who is also the other parent of your child is one of the most difficult kinds of relationship known. The therapist's sister had faced this kind of conflicted relationship firsthand. She had been the caretaker in her marriage also. She had earned most of the money, written all the checks, and so forth. Several years after the divorce, their house burned down, destroying all the children's possessions—furniture, clothes, toys, books, everything. When the mother filed the insurance claim, it was discovered that her ex-husband's name was still on the policy. He would have to sign the claim before any reimbursement could be made. He refused to do this.

When she pointed out to the insurance company that she had paid the premiums out of her own income for several years, they relented and offered to pay. But her ex-husband (a respected attorney, by the way) threatened to sue them if they did! He was willing to cause his children incredible hardship rather than cooperate with his ex-wife about *anything*. Furthermore, she still had to deal with him regarding child support, visitation, vacation, and so forth.

So when Anne talked about the contemptuous ways Walter treated her, she knew Lynn understood. For the sake of her children, Anne wanted to find some way to forgive Walter. Among other things, Lynn told Anne that forgiveness is a way to become powerful, a background against which one's own integrity can be lived out.

Lynn suggested that when Walter sent an impersonal memorandum, she could answer it with a friendly letter. When the kids repeated some insulting thing he had said about her, she could say nonchalantly, "Yeah, that's somewhat accurate. I was not a perfect wife or a perfect mother." When he was insulting to her, she could tune out the insult part of his comments and respond only to the rest. When he brought the kids home late, she could comment on what a good time they seemed to have had. She could be in charge of herself!

It took Anne a long time to change her reactions, but as she did, Walter seemed to change. His conversations became less abrasive. He started asking about visitation times rather than demanding them. He even wrote her a halfway friendly letter once. She was careful not to comment on the tone of the letter, but responded with a friendly letter of her own. If she had commented on the friendly tone of the letter, it might have sounded as if she was criticizing him for all the times when his letters were not friendly. Anne said she welcomed these small changes; but in a deeper sense, they were irrelevant. She was changing for *her,* not to try to make him change.

In her reflections a year or so later, Anne told her therapist that she kept thinking, "He is no longer my husband, but he is still the father of my children. If I criticize him to my children, I am hurting them. If I don't get along with him, I am hurting them. If I get defensive about the ways he treats me, I am hurting them. It is in my children's best interests for their father to be happy and successful!"

Rhonda had suffered all her adult life with chronic feelings of depression and worthlessness. One night, she saw a TV show about a woman remembering that she had been sexually abused by her father. Suddenly she realized that this is what had happened to her. Memories flooded her mind with unmistakable clarity.

The next day, she talked with her pastor, who listened gently and supportively, but also talked with her about the importance of forgiving. Rhonda struggled with this. She was too angry and hurt to think about forgiving. It felt almost like more abuse—she was being asked yet again to sacrifice her own well-being and integrity for the sake of her father.

So she consulted the pastoral counselor in her church. He supported her also, but told her the exact opposite of what the pastor told her. He told her that forgiveness is appropriate only if the offender has confessed and repented. He encouraged her to plan eventually to confront her father. Unless he was willing to take her seriously and deal with her openly, there could be no forgiveness, no authentic relationship.

But Rhonda had problems with this also. She knew her father would deny everything, accusing her of making it up or of being misled by those "therapist types." If she told others in the family, they would support the father, and she would be ostracized. She could see no way that confrontation would lead to anything other than horrible power struggles, in which everyone would lose.

So she consulted yet another pastoral counselor, Janice. Rhonda was a very spiritual person and emphasized that she wanted to deal with her father in a Christian way. Janice heard her out, listening to the conflicting advice she had been given, and reflected on how confusing all this must have been.

Rhonda insisted that Janice tell her God's will relative to forgiveness.

Janice stressed the difference between forgiveness and reconciliation. *Forgiveness* is internal, having to do with attitudes, priorities, and a willingness to take the first step. But *reconciliation* depends in large part on the other person. In some cases, you cannot have an authentic relationship with someone until he or she will deal with you about the terrible offenses he or she inflicted on you.

The first task is dealing with the inner self. Forgiveness at that level means regaining your own sense of self, your own self-esteem, your own integrity. It often involves grieving for the losses you suffered during that time—and since then. It will probably involve dealing with shame and anger. It means tapping into a deeper level of reality than the reality of the offenses, affirming the world of the spirit. To access that dimension is to forgive and, conversely, as we forgive, we gain easier access to that level.

Forgiveness at this level means to withdraw importance from the abuse, and give importance to the deeper realities. Perhaps this is an essential ingredient in all healing and growth.

Janice told Rhonda that after she did that, she could decide what to do about her father. Janice was a pragmatist, and did not believe in wasting time and energy trying something that was likely to make things worse. She knew that, at best, confrontations can be terribly disillusioning.

Healing and growth can take place in many ways. Much contemporary therapy is based on the idea that memories of traumatic events are often repressed. Young children simply do not have the resources to deal with some of the terrible things that can happen to them, so they repress the memories of these events. These memories still exist in the subconscious mind, and still influence the child, but since they are locked away, out of consciousness, they cannot be processed. They are not accessible to the adult resources the person now has. Therapy from this perspective consists of retrieving these memories and dealing with them as an adult.

Consider some other means of healing and growth. Healing often takes place at a subconscious level, without having to engage one's consciousness. Most of our psychological growth takes place this way, as a by-product of the processes of living. Psychiatrist Carl Whitaker stated that in therapy, insight *follows* healing and growth, rather than the other way around. Sometimes even the insight is superfluous. A well-known family therapist told me once that he had consulted psychiatrist Milton Erickson for one session of hypnotherapy many years ago. He said he had no memory of what happened, but for the next couple of years, he was aware of some significant changes in his life. Memories of past events do not necessarily need to be processed consciously.

As Rhonda's therapy progressed, she wondered if it were necessary to confront her father at all. She knew how defensive he was, but she also knew that in his own limited way, he truly loved her. If she confronted him, it would most certainly bring an end to whatever relationship they now had. Dad was old now, and physically frail. He was not the same person that he was thirty years ago, nor was she.

It is hard to say who had the power in their present relationship. For a long time now, issues of power had been somewhat ambiguous. She saw ways that Dad was dependent on her, often looking to her for approval and nurture. She realized that as long as her resentment was active, she was stuck in the one-down position of the victim.

When she began to forgive him, she began to feel powerful. Maybe it is not that the one with power forgives, but rather that when one forgives, one *becomes* powerful. To forgive presupposes an inner power and enhances it.

Janice spoke once of another client with similar circumstances. She did confront her father, who admitted that it was true and apologized in a casual, perfunctory manner. When she told him that was not enough, he asked caustically, "What do you want me to do, read a script?" She took that seriously, and spent a long time writing an appropriate script. She then asked her father for some time together one evening when everyone else was gone.

When he read the script, it was with obvious irritation, but he did read it. She thanked him warmly, saying she really appreciated his willingness to take her seriously. (An old Jewish proverb states "It is better to do a good deed from a bad motive than to refrain from doing the good deed because of the bad motive.") She also said she would like him to read it to her again at a later time.

The next time, the words seemed to be sinking in. When he read it to her a third time, another week later, he looked at her and said with deep feeling, "I'm so sorry."

The daughter said it was clear to her that her father would never have dropped his defensiveness unless he understood that she wanted to be reconciled with him, not to humiliate him. In this sense, the script was like a prayer of confession. The written words served as a vehicle for evoking the feelings that needed to be expressed.

One woman was in her sixties when she began to remember sexual abuse. Both of her parents had been dead for years. Throughout their lives, they had both been obsessed with their image as good parents. They had instilled that so deeply into their daughter that even now, she felt guilty talking about their imperfections.

When she had first consulted a psychologist, in her twenties, they were aghast at the thought that she might be telling him something about them, and exclaimed, "How could you do that to us?"

The current therapist reminded her that both parents were now dead and had therefore confronted God. They have had to answer to God for everything about their lives. They had experienced whatever judgment was appropriate and had also experienced healing and forgiveness in ways that only God can know. The therapist said

> If Mother and Dad could come back to you, they would tell you that they have made their peace with God, and their only concern now is for your well-being. "In spite of all our faults, we really do love you. We want what is best for you, no matter how badly it may reflect on us. Whatever you need to remember, we want you to remember it. No matter what you need to think or

feel about us, we want to do it. Our only concern now is for your well-being.

The woman wept while the therapist was saying this and asked him to repeat it, which he did. She then asked again, "What was it they said?" (not "What was it they *would have* said?").

Another woman wrote her father a letter in which she said she needed to let him know that she remembered the ways he had sexually abused her as a child. He might not even remember them, and she was not asking him to confess or even to acknowledge her letter. She was writing only because she needed to express what was in her heart. Her father did not acknowledge the letter, but she felt she had done what was necessary and could get on with her life.

A most remarkable incident was reported by Goldie Mae Bristol (1982, pp. 151-152). An incest survivor talked with her counselor about her bitter hatred toward her father. At one point, the counselor suggested that she ask her father to forgive her for her hatred! The woman was aghast at such a thought, but eventually, she did. Her father broke into tears and said he had longed for the day when they could talk.

In this situation, her father could not very well deny what he had done, because the daughter had not accused him of anything. She was not out to humiliate him. Her apology was a way of accepting the subordinate position for herself. She wanted healing, not revenge.

Personally, I can't imagine myself ever suggesting this to anyone. But in this situation, it was the woman's way of asserting her power.

Rhonda never did confront her father, but several times when they were together she said things that let him know that she remembered the abuse. He never commented on this, but she thought she detected a new quality of humility in him.

Chapter 17

Forgiving Myself:
Forgiving the Person I Used to Be

Unless you hang around with really mean people, the only one who will remember the stupid and petty things you have done is you.

Author unknown

Our capacity to be cruel to ourselves never ceases to amaze me.

Frank Ostaseski

Florence thought of herself as a very good nurse: bright, conscientious, caring. One morning, she noticed that her husband, Carl, seemed to be in some distress. When she asked him about it, he said he had been having abdominal pain for the past few days. This morning, it seemed to be worse. As he talked, a spasm of pain racked his body. He doubled over, face ashen, hands trembling, with sweat forming on his forehead. Florence rushed him to the doctor's office.

The doctor was very busy that morning. He took a quick look at Carl and said that he seemed to have the flu. He asked them to wait in a treatment room while his nurse took vital signs.

As a good nurse, Florence knew it was not the flu. It was obviously a serious problem—appendicitis at least, maybe worse, but she could not convince the doctor that her husband was seriously ill and needed immediate attention.

As a nurse, she had been taught always to defer to the doctor. That was a recurrent theme in her training. Besides, that was her own personality style. She found it very difficult to stand up for her own convictions and wishes. So instead of walking out of the doctor's office and going straight to the hospital, she waited and waited and waited.

Finally, some twenty minutes later, with her husband visibly worse, she took him to the hospital, where they did emergency surgery. Carl survived the surgery, but his system had been seriously weakened. After several days, he took a turn for the worse, and fell into a coma.

When Florence saw him, she knew he was going to die. She also knew that the time she had wasted in the doctor's office was partly—maybe largely—responsible for the coma. If only she had had enough initiative and courage, Carl would not now be dying. How could she ever forgive herself?

One friend tried to minimize her responsibility. How can a wife who is overwhelmed with anxiety be expected to make appropriate evaluations and decisions? It was a tragedy, not a crime. She should not blame herself. When stressed, she was just not herself, not the person who usually handles things so well.

Another friend pointed out that other people were more to blame than she was. Carl waited several days before telling her about his pain. Was that his pride, his macho stance? Even if he had sought medical treatment at the very first sign of pain, there was no guarantee he would have lived.

It was partly the doctor's fault. He was the authority and should have taken charge of the situation immediately. He had no right to dismiss her concern simply because she was distraught.

The hospital may have been partly responsible. Who knows what mistakes or oversights might have occurred? If Carl's condition had been monitored more carefully, might not that have made a difference?

Florence dismissed all of these observations as rationalizations. She could not block from her mind the conviction that her weakness, her characterological defects, had in effect killed her husband.

For a long time, she looked for ways to atone for this terrible thing. But how? There was no way she could make it up to him or to their family. No restitution was possible. She couldn't fill his shoes as a father to their children. She was already a devoted mother and did not know what more she could do.

On the other hand, she knew she could not carry this guilt for the rest of her life, or she would destroy her family and herself. She had very little energy or inclination to engage her children. What value could there be in punishing herself so severely or in suppressing all pleasure and satisfaction?

A profound difference exists between innocence and forgiveness. Florence's friends wanted to restore her innocence, to tell her in various ways that it was not her fault. Florence knew she was not innocent. She was a flawed, defective human being. Nothing could change that; nothing could restore her innocence.

Ellen faced a somewhat similar situation. While she was still in college, she became pregnant and had an abortion. The aftermath was a horrible, pervading sense of guilt. Eventually she married the man who had impregnated her and they had another child. Nevertheless, the guilt continued, and it became clear to Ellen that her guilt was interfering with her mothering of the child she now had. Deep in her heart, she felt that if she loved the child she now had, she was being disloyal to the child she had killed (for Ellen, it was a child, not a fetus).

Her friends tried to tell her it was not her fault: she was under an enormous amount of stress; she wasn't really herself; her options were all unacceptable to her; most people would have made the same painful choice she did.

But Ellen, just as Florence, dismissed these observations as irrelevant to her own values. In her eyes, she was terribly guilty. How could she ever forgive herself? (see Close, 1988).

I could understand Florence's and Ellen's dilemmas. I felt the same way about myself. On the one hand, I berated myself for my stupidity. On the other hand, I knew that when I did that, I made life harder for myself.

At some level, I knew that forgiving myself and forgiving Alexander must go hand in hand. If I could ever simply accept the fact that I am imperfect, and imperfect people make mistakes, it would be easier to forgive Alexander. Conversely, if I could see Alexander as other than the incarnation of evil, it would be easier to forgive myself. I was seeing both myself and him as one-dimensional: I was an idiot for lending him money; he was a traitor for not repaying it.

If I could find some value in this mistake, it would be easier to forgive myself. That value would be in what I could learn, especially in what I could learn about myself.

I have often told clients that a personal failure, such as divorce, is like a postgraduate course in human relations. It is a course for which they paid a very high tuition. They should learn everything it had to teach.

So what could I learn? What was my subconscious mind trying to teach me in relation to my friend Alexander?

To some extent, my loan was an affirmation of our friendship. An important ingredient of a friendship is the exchange of favors. You do something for me; I do something for you. That affirms our equality and our trust in each other.

Problems arise if the exchange gets off balance. I may do big favors for you, and you do only small ones for me. I may do many favors for you, although you do very few for me. Then it is no longer a balanced relationship. It has become dependency oriented.

My lending money to Alexander was a big favor—a bigger one than he had ever done me. I think he immediately put me in the role of benefactor, or parent, rather than friend. A parent is supposed to give without any thought of being repaid.

Related to this is the possibility that I was trying to ingratiate my-self with Alexander, to obligate him to me. Did that mean that my self-esteem was at a low ebb, and I didn't think he could like me just for me? Did I need to buy his friendship? If that was the case, I was horribly mistaken.

To what extent did I want to feel magnanimous, be a big shot? Was this my way of feeling important? Was I showing off how generous I could be? If so, why? To what extent was I being grandiose, blissfully assuming that anything I did would turn out all right? Do I not need to exercise the caution that other people do?

To what extent did I lend this money because it is difficult for me to say no? I have learned a lot about saying no over the years. I even wrote an article about it. But it is still difficult at times. Somebody's request touches some vulnerable spot in me, and I act against my better judgment. Sometimes it seems that I have an almost pathologi-cal need to please people.

When I could not forgive myself, was I buying into the delusion that money is everything? Was I basing my life too much on the idea that money equals freedom, money equals worth, money brings hap-piness? Was losing money an unforgivable sin?

Was I primarily distressed because I had made a fool of myself and damaged my image?

I have friends who have made stupid mistakes. That did not affect our relationship. I did not think less of them. Sometimes, I was relieved to know they were as fallible as I am. Why was it so hard for me to offer myself the same sympathy and support I offered my friends? Am I not as worthy of the same forgiveness I would show a friend? Or am I so grandiose that I feel I should be perfect?

I don't like to think that any of those ideas are characteristic of me, but I know they are, sometimes more than others. If I can actually take them seriously, and not rationalize them away, I may be able to change. I may need to keep some of my guilt and shame to monitor what I do—not too much guilt and shame, but enough. Maybe someday I won't need those painful reminders. For now, I think I do.

I referred earlier to Robert Jay Lifton's study of the Nazi doctors. As I read his book, I was struck by the lack of remorse shown by these doctors. I did not get the sense that in their living, they felt a responsibility to atone for the atrocities in which they had participated.

Had they faced the darkness within and found some way to forgive themselves? Or did they merely excuse themselves? Did they live in denial, minimizing the suffering they had inflicted? Did they blame everything on orders from their superiors, as other Nazis had done when confronted with their evil? Did they convince themselves that the self who did those things was not the real self? The real self was the one who was now practicing medicine as a respected member of the community. Did they feel nothing was to be gained by keeping the memory of those times before them? Did any of them go into therapy? Did they make any effort to apologize or make restitution?

A German family was serving as missionaries to New Zealand when World War II broke out. As German nationals, they spent the duration in a detention camp. After the war, they returned to Germany, only to discover what their nation had done to the Jews. The son, Martin, now a young man, was particularly upset and consulted a therapist. At one point, he told his therapist that he felt a need to meet a Jew somewhere and apologize for what his countrymen had done.

The therapist asked him, "Do you not recognize my name?"

Without any conscious awareness of what he had done, Martin had chosen a Jewish therapist to help him with his shame, a Jewish therapist to whom he would open his heart, a Jewish therapist to whom he would confess on behalf of his countrymen.

Did any of the Nazi doctors take their guilt that seriously? Or did they tell themselves that what was past was past? They could not undo what they had done, so why dwell on it? Would any value be realized in facing that side of themselves?

When I was a young clergyman/therapist, I thought of guilt as negative, as an impediment. That was the prevailing mentality of the time. It was thought that if a person could just forgive himself or herself, that would free him or her to be a truly loving, productive human being. Self-forgiveness was essential.

I no longer think that all self-forgiveness is essential. In some circumstances, yes, but for many others, no. Many times people need the pressure of a realistic guilt for a variety of purposes.

Guilt can help us to monitor our behavior. Habits die slowly, even after the situations that created them have disappeared. A boy in school becomes a clever put-down artist as a way of dealing with his sense of inferiority. As an adult, he may outgrow that feeling of inferiority, but the abrasiveness may remain. If he can feel guilty about the demeaning ways he treats other people, that may be an important stimulus to his personal growth.

A young wife became promiscuous as a way of dealing with her husband's infidelities. She left that marriage and is now married to a man who is totally loyal to her (or as a friend said, "loyal to himself in relation to her"). She continues to have affairs, however. Guilt might be very valuable for her. Given the reality of AIDS, it might save her life and the life of her husband.

Guilt, like all other distressing feelings, can be thought of as oriented primarily to the future and only secondarily to the past. "I am guilty *in order to* . . ." is more important than, "I am guilty *because of* . . ."

The inner self, the subconscious mind, is always working for our well-being, as it understands that. If the inner self creates guilt within us, it is worth asking, "What do I need to do differently? Is this guilt there for some constructive purpose?" When we have heeded the voice of our guilt, then it is no longer needed. Until that time, it may be very useful.

Some members of a therapy group for men who had sexually abused their daughters said that when they were caught, they went to their pastors and confessed. Without exception, the pastors assured them that they were forgiven.

The men were emphatic in affirming that this was *not* helpful. To be forgiven so blithely relieved them of the need to take their problems seriously. It relieved them of the need to deal with their daughters about the terrible things they had done to them. It took away some of the pressure they needed to stay in therapy. At that point in their recovery, they needed the pressure. To take their pathology seriously, they needed to feel guilty.

For many of us, self-forgiveness needs to be at the *end* of the healing/growth process, not at the beginning. When as a young therapist I tried to relieve people of their guilt, I was presuming to know more about what was best for them than their inner selves knew.

Does this kind of guilt arise from the naive assumption that life is simple, or that if we live well, we will not be called on to make difficult decisions? Does it arise from the grandiose idea that we should handle all situations superbly? Irrational guilt can help us realize what it means to be imperfect human beings, muddling our way through life like everybody else. Guilt in such situations confronts us with the complexity of life.

Keep as much guilt as you need to make sure you do not treat others (or yourself) badly. Other motivations, such as self-esteem and integrity, will take the place of guilt as you continue to grow. There will be a time to leave the guilt behind, but if you need guilt now, keep it. Don't keep more than you need, but it is probably better to keep too much than too little.

Forgiving myself, as with forgiving another person, is both outward and inward. Outwardly, I deliberately renounce revenge. In relation to myself, this means that I will interrupt the times I am berating myself. I may say something like, "Damn, there I go again," and deliberately shift my attention elsewhere—such as getting together with a trusted friend.

Inwardly, forgiveness means letting go of resentment and looking for healing. In relation to myself, this means tapping into deeper levels of spirituality. I find deeper levels of freedom, of self-esteem, and of intimacy.

The two foundations for forgiving myself are similar to those for forgiving another person.

I forgive another person by changing the way I define my world; I give importance to things other than the offense.

I also forgive by realizing that the offender is multidimensional. He or she is not totally characterized by any one aspect. Neither am I. I am more than just the part that sometimes offends, and I need to access those other facets of my personality.

I know that forgiving another person or myself is much easier if I feel connected to people who love me. So when I felt I was ready to forgive myself, I reconnected with some of my close friends. We had lunch together or otherwise got together to talk. I told them what I was struggling with and that their friendship was especially important to me now.

An unusual experience helped me immensely in the process of forgiving myself. I attended a performance of Mahler's Third Symphony. When I walked into the auditorium, I was still carrying much of the burden of my stupidity. When I left, I had left much of it behind. I don't know how to explain that. Maybe my understandings set the stage, and the symphony brought the healing to the surface. Maybe in the presence of music so magnificent, so awesome, my mistakes seemed utterly trivial. Maybe it was something else. I just know it was a redemptive experience.

Chapter 18

Painting Lessons

[D]efining myself by those who affirm me, not by those who demean me.

People often feel guilt or shame, even when no wrongdoing occurs. A man finally takes charge of a deteriorating family situation and puts his mother in a nursing home. He knows he has no alternative but feels profoundly guilty. An elderly man may have instructed his family to take no heroic measures to keep him alive, but when faced with the actual situation, his loved ones can feel very guilty.

The aftermath of childhood sexual abuse is often an overwhelming sense of guilt as well as shame. I first met Helen when she was a patient at the state mental hospital where I was chaplain. She had been sexually abused as a child, and felt it was all her fault.

Helen functioned fairly well into her mid-teens. Then something happened to trigger her memories, and she became seriously suicidal. Before her admission to the hospital, she had cut her wrists several times and taken several overdoses of medication. On one occasion, such an overdose left her unconscious for three days.

Helen's uncle had told her that she was responsible for the sexual activity. He had only tried to help her. At some deep level, Helen believed him.

Does this mean Helen really was to blame? Of course not. She was a child, a very vulnerable child. She trusted her uncle and submitted to him as a way of addressing her loneliness. He took cruel advantage of her vulnerability. It was he who was to blame.

Helen would not accept that understanding. She was convinced that she was primarily responsible. She could not think of herself as innocent. She could not forgive herself.

I told Helen that if she wished to think that way, that was up to her. I thought of it differently. I thought she should assess very carefully the amount of blame that was realistically hers and the amount that more appropriately fell on her uncle's shoulders. I didn't know whether her responsibility was one one hundredth of 1 percent, or maybe as much as two one hundredths of 1 percent, certainly no more than that. It was grandiose and self-centered to accept more responsibility than was rightfully hers. On one occasion, I told her a story.

There was once a young woman who had been given a beautiful painting of an adolescent girl, bright eyed and eager as she faced her life and her thrilling future. But someone had defaced this picture. He had painted an evil horrible man in the background, with a gnarled ugly hand across the girl's face, obscuring her beauty and her pleasure in living.

The young woman did not know what to do with this painting. It was certainly too ugly to let anyone see. She thought of throwing it away, and several times she actually took it out to the trash pile. Once she left it there for three whole days before retrieving it. On another occasion a friend found it on the trash pile with a couple of holes poked in it. She took it back to the young woman and suggested she take painting lessons.

Finally she took this advice. She began to learn about colors and pigments, and how to mix the different pigments to get the desired shades. She learned about brushes and strokes and how to move one's hand. She learned about light and shadows, perspective and composition. When she felt she had learned enough, she took the painting and began to study it very carefully.

Her first reactions were disgust and then a kind of fright. She felt it would be easy to feel overwhelmed by the task before her. But she persevered.

She started by repairing the damage that the canvas had suffered when it was on the trash pile. Next she bought some paint and brushes. She mixed the pigments very carefully, and painted over the evil person and the ugly hand that obscured the face of the girl.

To her dismay, the dark pigments of this evil man started seeping through the new paint. Try as she might, she could not cover up that malignant influence. She was discouraged for a while, but finally tried something else.

Very carefully she took a razor blade and started scraping away the pigment that defined the ugliness.

At first she scraped very tentatively, getting only the surface of the ugliness. But as time progressed, she scraped more confidently. Sometimes she would scrape away just a little bit, revealing the color of the girl's skin.

Sometimes she became impatient, and scraped so vigorously she actually scraped away some of the underlying pigment that defined the girl. It left the painting marred and incomplete. On a couple occasions, she scraped so vigorously she actually tore the underlying canvas, and had to stop and repair it. But she was so pleased at being rid of the ugliness that she didn't mind the damage.

She would then take her paints and brushes, mix the pigments carefully to get the desired colors and shades, and fill in the places that had been damaged.

Finally she finished. Her skills as a painter had not been terribly good, so the finished product did not look as beautiful as if it had not been damaged. Instead of a dreamlike innocence, there was now a rugged, hardy feel to the painting, that was actually very appealing. She was proud to hang it in her living room.

After she hung it up, she noticed a few dark spots she had missed, and some small areas where the dark pigment still leaked through. She managed to scrape away a few of the dark flecks with her fingernail, and touched up some of the discolored spots. But she decided it would be more trouble than it was worth to try to make it absolutely perfect. She had other things she wanted to do with her time and energy. She now wanted just to enjoy this painting and share its beauty and strength with the people she loved and who loved her. (Close, 1998, pp. 53-57)

Helen wept softly as I spoke, and thanked me warmly for the story. I felt this was one small step in the process of healing. Helen's growth was not instantaneous, but she did recover from the shame and the guilt—she forgave herself. She is now a respected therapist, who can walk very knowledgeably with other people along the sometimes rocky path of self-forgiveness.

Epilogue

The concept of forgiveness is often used in a broad sense.

Robert's early life had been quite difficult. He was only five when his father died, and his mother had to work two jobs to hold the family together. By some very hard work, she saw every one of her children through high school and college—all except Robert. He was the youngest and was most affected by the loss of his father. As the youngest, he also missed out on some very important mothering when he needed it the most.

Robert reacted to this by failing at everything he undertook. He dropped out of high school, got involved in drugs and alcohol, and committed a series of petty crimes. While he was in prison his wife took their three children and left him.

Finally Robert got his act together. He finished high school, then college, then theological seminary, and was ordained as a minister.

In his first church, Robert met and fell in love with a lovely woman and married her. Jenna had a child from a previous marriage who was now about nine years old. Ruthie had had Mom all to herself for some years, and she did not want some stranger coming between them. She did everything she could to break them up. She snapped at Robert, pouted at him, turned a cold shoulder to everything he tried to do with her. She wouldn't even accept a gift from him.

Robert was wise enough by this time to know that the best thing was to do nothing, but he knew that he had failed at being a father once before, and every time Ruthie was nasty to him, it reminded him of all his past failures.

One day there was a school picnic for kids and their parents. At one point, Ruthie came over to introduce a friend to her mother. Robert, as was his custom, stepped back to let Ruthie have center stage. She and her friend talked with Jenna for some moments.

Robert said that then Ruthie turned to him, and said to her friend, with a kind of shy warmth in her voice, "This is my daddy."

He said he managed not to cry, but those few words were overwhelming. He couldn't explain it logically, but what he *felt* in the depth of his heart was that he had been forgiven (adapted from Close, 1984, p. 82f).

A somewhat similar experience was reported by the author Antoine de Saint Exupéry, who was also one of the pioneers of French aviation. On one occasion, he and his copilot crash-landed in the Sahara Desert (the setting for *The Little Prince*), and wandered aimlessly for four days before being spotted by men in a camel caravan. His reflections are quite poignant.

> You, Bedouin of Libya who saved our lives, though you will dwell for ever in my memory, yet I shall never be able to recapture your features. You are Humanity and your face comes into my mind simply as man incarnate. You, our beloved fellow-man, did not know who we might be, and yet you recognized us without fail. And I, in my turn, shall recognize you in the faces of all mankind. You came towards me in an aureole of charity and magnanimity bearing the gift of water. All my friends and all my enemies marched towards me in your person. It did not seem to me that you were rescuing me; rather did it seem that you were forgiving me. And I felt I had no enemy left in all the world. (Saint Exupéry, 1992, p. 235)

Appendix A

Handling the Accusation of Incest

It is always easier to make things worse than to make them better.

It has become clear in recent years that sexual abuse in families is not a rare occurrence. Anyone is capable of abusing if he or she is physically or emotionally stronger than the victim. The more common situation is a father molesting his daughter. Fathers have also molested their young sons, and mothers have molested both sons and daughters. Other family members as well as neighbors and strangers have been guilty of sexual abuse.

Another kind of molesting is more common than the physical acts of sex. Many parents relate seductively to their children without ever touching them sexually. If a marriage is strained, it may be easy for a parent to place a child in the role of the significant other. Sometimes this may be harmless, but it is usually experienced by the child as terribly abusive.

Many therapists have specialized in treating incest survivors. Sometimes they get carried away in their zeal to support the client. They may tell the client that she (rarely he) shows all the signs of sexual abuse. They will then try to get the client to "remember."

People who consult a therapist are often extremely vulnerable. They may take the therapist's diagnosis as a revelation from God. If they come to believe they have been abused, it is easy for the subconscious mind to create "memories" that justify that belief. I don't know how often this happens. Sexual abuse is not rare, but there seem to be many cases of "false memory syndrome" also.

Many daughters are now confronting their fathers, accusing them of sexual abuse. Much has been written about this. But very little has been written about how fathers can handle this accusation. How is forgiveness relevant in this situation?

Some fathers have acknowledged the abuse, with deep and sincere apologies. Many were grateful that it was finally brought out into the open. They have taken full responsibility, and affirmed their love for their daughters. One father even said that he had no right to ask for his daughter's forgiveness. This kind of response is the most likely to promote healing and reconciliation.

Daughters often want to forgive their fathers and have a relationship with them. The more open a father can be about his abuse, the more open the daughter is to forgiving and resuming a relationship. By admitting the abuse, the father is saying, "I am not now the same man I was then."

Other fathers have admitted the abuse but minimized its extent or its importance. One elderly father admitted fondling his daughters but angrily denounced them for accusing him of having had intercourse with them.

This set up a power struggle that no one could possibly win. If the daughter submitted to her father's assertions, she would be denying her own self. If the father submitted to the daughter's accusations, he would be compromising the image of himself he wanted to convey—which he could not do. Being thought of as innocent was more important than being forgiven. He died a few years later, alienated from his entire family.

Some fathers have admitted the sexual behavior but said in various ways that it was the daughter's fault. She led him on, or she liked the sex, or he was just teaching her about life, or it was a secret that made them special to each other. Most daughters experience this as yet another instance of abuse.

Other fathers have angrily denied the accusations. They often attribute these accusations to the daughter's malice or pathology, or to a therapist's influence. When a man does this, he is implying, "I have not changed. I am still the same man I was then."

The mother is inevitably caught in the middle of this struggle, having to choose between her husband and her daughter. Often the daughter will insist that her mother leave the father because of what he has done.

If a daughter has had good psychotherapy, she may forgive this kind of father. However, she will probably never be able to trust him, and she will certainly not want him around her children.

Whenever a daughter thinks she has been abused by her father, I assume she is correct, but the abuse may have been emotional rather than physical. We human beings often create "memories" that express emotional truths. A daughter may be right about the abuse, but may be mistaken about its form. She remembers *feeling* abused and assumes she was physically abused. Her father knows he did not touch her physically and is therefore "innocent."

It is not the physical sexual acts that are so damaging. It is the sense of being used. It is the violation of generational boundaries, being forced to grow up too fast, being exploited. These violations can occur even when no physical sexual abuse occurred. So the term "sexual abuse" may symbolize those other realities. The apology that is asked of a father is not just for the act of intercourse, it is for a stance that the daughter has experienced as abusive.

One father wanted to take his daughter's accusations seriously, but he had no memories of anything resembling abuse. Joe and Patricia are both in their late sixties and in poor health. Patricia describes their forty-three years of marriage as rocky, but with an underlying sense of commitment and love. Celia, now thirty-five and unmarried, is their only child.

Celia, who lives in another state, has been in therapy for two years. She recently wrote her father and angrily accused him of having sex with her during a family vacation when she was twelve. Joe told her it was hard for him to imagine that he could have done such a thing. He has a very good memory for the past, often with minute details, and says he is sure if he had done that, he would remember it.

Celia rejects that, and insists that he confess. She also wants her mother to leave Joe. At that point, Joe consulted me, asking if hypnosis could help him remember. I did not regard formal hypnosis as appropriate and suggested he and his wife come together for a family consultation.

Joe and Patricia seem older than their ages, devoted to their daughter and eager for healing. If he did molest Celia, Joe wants to remember it so he can apologize meaningfully.

There are several perspectives on a situation such as this:

1. The fallibility of memory. There is no way to know for sure what happened twenty-three years ago. Besides, this is a problem in the present, not in the past. Celia's concerns affect her life in the here and now. To focus on the past is to misunderstand.

2. The power imbalance. Children grow up with their parents having much more power than they. Hopefully, in adulthood, that power imbalance evens out. Children no longer feel subordinate to their parents. This is easier if the parents will validate their children's maturity. But in many families, the imbalance persists for many years.

An act of incest is an extreme example of the imbalance of power. When a daughter accuses her father, she is at one level trying to equalize the power. If her father accepts her accusation, he is acknowledging her power. If he angrily rejects it, he is assuming a dominant stance relative to her, which will increase her need to equalize the power.

3. Since Celia has chosen to make this accusation by letter rather than by phone or in person, the parents should honor her chosen way of communication by *writing* back rather than telephoning. When one is *speaking* to another, part of the listener's energy goes into listening, and part goes into thinking of a reply. In a letter, a person can devote more attention to understanding the other's point of view.

In the letter, her father can say that *he accepts her memory of the situation* even though he has no memory of it. He knows he made many mistakes as a parent—many serious mistakes. He can only apologize to her from the bottom of his heart for these. He will do whatever he can to promote healing and hopes someday she will be able to forgive him for all of his inadequacies.

If the daughter insists that he acknowledge sexual abuse, her father can reiterate his acceptance of her memory, even though he does not remember.

4. The mother is also in an extremely difficult situation. If she accepts her daughter's memory, she alienates her husband; if she does not do as her daughter asks, she alienates her daughter.

One way out of this dilemma might be for Mom to approach her relationships with her daughter and with her husband separately. Mom can accept her daughter's view *in relation to the daughter.* She can ask, "What do you want me to do *in relation to you?*" She can also accept Joe's view of the situation *in relation to Joe.* That way, she may be able to stay out of the middle and not get caught up in the power struggle.

I'm certainly not suggesting that this is easy, or that it is guaranteed to help, but it might be one to approach an extremely difficult situation.

One final word for the person accused of sexual abuse. What your child needs is your humility, not a lecture on the fallibility of memory. A lecture automatically puts you in a dominant position and reinforces the very thing you are trying to negate. The ideas I have expressed here are addressed to *you.* They are not intended as insight for your child. I hope these thoughts will help *you* approach your child with humility. If you quote to your child anything I have written here, I guarantee that it will make things worse!

Appendix B

Kinds of Offenses

I. *Offenses against freedom,* which limit my ability to make choices (abuses of power, leaving me feeling impotent, trapped, and helpless):
   A. Trivial: inconvenience
   B. Moderate: coercion, control, exploitation, oppression
   C. Catastrophic: enslavement

II. *Offenses against self-esteem,* which undercut my need to be valued (abuses of importance, leaving me feeling worthless):
   A. Trivial: slights
   B. Moderate: criticism, insult
   C. Catastrophic: humiliation

III. *Offenses against intimacy,* which interfere with my ability to love and to be loved (abuses of trust, leaving me feeling desolate and abandoned):
   A. Trivial: indifference
   B. Moderate: rejection, disloyalty
   C. Catastrophic: betrayal

Within this framework, there are five other factors:

1. *Importance:* Was the offense trivial, moderate, or catastrophic? A trivial offense leaves me bruised, and I can usually ignore that. A moderate offense leaves me injured, and I can recover from that. A catastrophic offense leaves me crippled. I may survive, but life will never be the same.
2. *Proximity:* Was the person who offended me a stranger, an acquaintance, or a friend or loved one? Many offenses are committed by strangers. Some of them are accidental, such as dialing a wrong telephone number. Some are simply inconsiderate, such as someone butting in line. Some are generic, and I simply happen to be at the wrong

place at the wrong time, such as, for instance, if I were a robbery victim. But some offenses are directed against me personally by someone who is important to me, designed to hurt: An acquaintance seeks revenge; a friend spreads malicious gossip; a loved one contemptuously rejects me.

3. *Intention:* Was the offense deliberate, something done against me personally to hurt me? Or was it the result of a characterological flaw in the offender, and I just happened to be in the way? Or was it accidental?

4. *Power:* Am I the offender's equal, subordinate, or superior?

5. *The nature of the offense:* Was it simply an act of some kind, or was the offense deeper than that, having to do with the character or personality of the offender and his or her relation to me? Was it a sin of commission ("You insulted me!"), or was it a sin of omission ("You ignored me!")? To what extent did the offense imply that I deserved to be treated badly? If so, does that mean the offender took it on himself or herself to make that judgment, and then execute it? Perhaps the most devastating aspect of abuse is the implication, "You deserve to be abused!" Boxers hit each other without creating emotional devastation, but not so with spouses. But of course boxers enter these situations voluntarily; spouses usually do not.

All of these distinctions are academic; in real life, they overlap and become blurred. Perhaps they are best thought of as levels of injury, or different facets of an offense.

Bibliographic Essay

Many good books on forgiveness have been published. I can't begin to list them all here. I would encourage you to check two or three at a time out of the library. Browse through them to see if they address your concerns in ways that are helpful to you. When you find books that you like, read them carefully.

The only book I regard as essential is Viktor Frankl's moving account of his concentration camp experiences (*Man's Search for Meaning,* New York: Washington Square Press, 1985). I regard this as one of the most important books ever written. It is a must for anyone interested in forgiveness.

Two books by Lewis Smedes (*Forgive and Forget,* San Francisco: Harper and Row, 1984; and *The Art of Forgiving,* Nashville: Moorings, 1996) are well-written, thoughtful, and compelling.

I also enjoyed Nicholas Tavuchis' *Mea Culpa: The Sociology of Apology* (Stanford University Press, 1991). This book is rather academic, but I include it because you are unlikely to encounter it in your library searches.

Another book you may not come upon is Donald Shriver's *An Ethic for Enemies* (New York: Oxford University Press, 1995). This is rather heavy reading, but I found it worth the effort.

If you are a scholar, you will want to read Hannah Arendt's very brief discussion of forgiveness. She regards it as an essential remedy for the irreversibility of the past. The ability to make and keep promises is similarly the remedy for the unpredictability of the future (*The Human Condition,* Chicago: University of Chicago Press, 1958, Chapter V, sections 33 and 34).

Rabbi Harold Kushner has a fine chapter on revenge ("Wild Justice: The Seductive Pleasure of Getting Even," pp. 60-85) in his book *Living a Life that Matters* (New York: Alfred Knopf, 2001).

Dr. Deborah Tannen's book *You Just Don't Understand* (New York: Ballantine Books, 1987) discusses how men and women communicate differently. I think it is a valuable contribution to any discussion of human relationships.

An interesting article on forgiveness appeared in the religion section of *Time* magazine, April 5, 1999 by David van Biema titled "Should All Be Forgiven?" (pp. 55-58). Another excellent article in *Time*, January 20, 2003 by Laura Koss-Feder is titled "Patching It Up." (pp. A7-A8).

My article "Symmetry and Complementarity," is relevant to the discussion of forgiveness. It was originally published in the *Journal of Pastoral Care*, Fall, 1992, and was reprinted in my book *Metaphor in Psychotherapy* (Atascadero, CA: Impact Publishers, 1998, Chapter 23).

Dr. Fred Luskin has developed a program on forgiveness at Stanford University. His book, *Forgive for Good,* is based on this program and incorporates some of the same principles I have described in this book. (Harper San Francisco, 2002).

References

Augsburger, David (1996). *Helping People Forgive*. Louisville, KY: John Knox Press.

Beyer/Amman, Lisa (1999). The Price of Honor. *Time,* January 18.

Bridges, Ruby (2000). The Education of Ruby Nell, *Guideposts,* March.

Bristol, Goldie with Carol McGinnis (1982). *When It's Hard to Forgive*. Wheaton, IL: Victor Books.

Close, Henry (1984). A Blessing for Me. In Gregory Johanson, ed., *Feed My Sheep*. New York: Paulist Press.

_____(1988). A Funeral for an Aborted Baby. *VOICES: The Art and Science of Psychotherapy* (Spring) 24(1): 66-69.

_____(1998). *Metaphor in Psychotherapy: Clinical Applications of Stories and Allegories*. Atascadero, CA: Impact Publishers, Inc.

Coles, Robert (1997). *The Moral Intelligence of Children*. New York: Random House.

Dobson, Terry (1982). Epilogue: A Safe Answer. From *Safe and Alive* (pp. 128-132). New York: Jeremy P. Tarcher, an imprint of Penguin Putnam, Inc.

Frankl, Viktor E. (1985). *Man's Search for Meaning*. New York: Washington Square Press. Originally published as *From Death-Camp to Existentialism: A Psychiatrist's Path to a New Therapy*. Boston: Beacon Press, 1959.

Keene, Frederick (1992). Structures of forgiveness in the New Testament. Unpublished paper. San Bernardino, CA.

Lifton, Robert Jay (1988). *The Nazi Doctors*. New York: Basic Books.

Morris, Debbie (1998). *Forgiving the Dead Man Walking*. Grand Rapids, MI: Zondervan Press.

Paris, Erna (1985). *Unhealed Wounds: France and the Klaus Barbie Affair*. New York: Grove Press.

Patton, John (1985). *Is Human Forgiveness Possible?* Nashville, TN: Abingdon Press.

Saint Exupéry, Antoine de (1992). *Wind, Sand, and Stars*. New York: Harcourt, Inc. Originally published 1939.

Schmidt, Ruth (1993). After the Fact: To Speak of Rape. *The Christian Century,* January 6-13, pp. 14-17.

van Biema, David (1999). Should All Be Forgiven? *Time,* April 5, pp. 55-58.

Wiesenthal, Simon (1998). *The Sunflower: On the Possibilities and Limits of Forgiveness*. New York: Schocken Press.

THE HAWORTH PASTORAL PRESS®
Pastoral Care, Ministry, and Spirituality
Richard Dayringer, ThD
Senior Editor

BECOMING A FORGIVING PERSON: A PASTORAL PERSPECTIVE by Henry Close. *"Becoming A Forgiving Person* is a tender and compelling work that charts differing paths which lead to personal healing through the medium of forgiveness. Close's wisdom of psyche and soul come together in very practical ways through his myriad stories and illustrations." *Virginia Felder, MDiv, ThM, DMin, Licensed Professional Counselor, Licensed Marriage and Family Therapist, Private Practice, Dallas, TX*

A PASTORAL COUNSELOR'S MODEL FOR WELLNESS IN THE WORK-PLACE: PSYCHERGONOMICS by Robert L. Menz. "This text is a must-read for chaplains and pastoral counselors wishing to understand and apply holistic health care to troubled employees, whether they be nurses, physicians, other health care workers, or workers in other industries. This book is filled with practical ideas and tools to help clergy care for the physical, mental, and spiritual needs of employees at the workplace." *Harold G. Koenig, MD, Associate Professor of Psychiatry, Duke University Medical Center; Author,* Chronic Pain: Biomedical and Spiritual Approaches

A THEOLOGY OF PASTORAL PSYCHOTHERAPY: GOD'S PLAY IN SACRED SPACES by Brian W. Grant. "Brian Grant's book is a compassionate and sophisticated synthesis of theology and psychoanalysis. His wise, warm grasp binds a community of healers with the personal qualities, responsibilities, and burdens of the pastoral psychotherapist." *David E. Scharff, MD, Co-Director, International Institute of Object Relations Therapy*

LOSSES IN LATER LIFE: A NEW WAY OF WALKING WITH GOD, SECOND EDITION by R. Scott Sullender. "Continues to be a timely and helpful book. There is an empathetic tone throughout, even though the book is a bold challenge to grieve for the sake of growth and maturity and faithfulness. . . . An important book." *Herbert Anderson, PhD, Professor of Pastoral Theology, Catholic Theological Union, Chicago, Illinois*

CARING FOR PEOPLE FROM BIRTH TO DEATH edited by James E. Hightower Jr. "An expertly detailed account of the hopes and hazards folks experience at each stage of their lives. Your empathy will be deepened and your care of people will be highly informed." *Wayne E. Oates, PhD, Professor of Psychiatry Emeritus, School of Medicine, University of Louisville, Kentucky*

HIDDEN ADDICTIONS: A PASTORAL RESPONSE TO THE ABUSE OF LEGAL DRUGS by Bridget Clare McKeever. "This text is a must-read for physicians, pastors, nurses, and counselors. It should be required reading in every seminary and Clinical Pastoral Education program." *Martin C. Helldorfer, DMin, Vice President, Mission, Leadership Development and Corporate Culture, Catholic Health Initiatives—Eastern Region, Pennsylvania*

THE EIGHT MASKS OF MEN: A PRACTICAL GUIDE IN SPIRITUAL GROWTH FOR MEN OF THE CHRISTIAN FAITH by Frederick G. Grosse. "Thoroughly grounded in traditional Christian spirituality and thoughtfully aware of the needs of men in our culture. . . . Close attention could make men's groups once again a vital spiritual force in the church." *Eric O. Springsted, PhD, Chaplain and Professor of Philosophy and Religion, Illinois College, Jacksonville, Illinois*

THE HEART OF PASTORAL COUNSELING: HEALING THROUGH RELATION-SHIP, REVISED EDITION by Richard Dayringer. "Richard Dayringer's revised edition of *The Heart of Pastoral Counseling* is a book for every person's pastor and a pastor's every person." *Glen W. Davidson, Professor, New Mexico Highlands University, Las Vegas, New Mexico*

WHEN LIFE MEETS DEATH: STORIES OF DEATH AND DYING, TRUTH AND COURAGE by Thomas W. Shane. "A kaleidoscope of compassionate, artfully tendered pastoral encounters that evoke in the reader a full range of emotions." *The Rev. Dr. James M. Harper, III, Corporate Director of Clinical Pastoral Education, Health Midwest; Director of Pastoral Care, Baptist Medical Center and Research Medical Center, Kansas City Missouri*

A MEMOIR OF A PASTORAL COUNSELING PRACTICE by Robert L. Menz. "Challenges the reader's belief system. A humorous and abstract book that begs to be read again, and even again." *Richard Dayringer, ThD, Professor and Director, Program in Psychosocial Care, Department of Medical Humanities; Professor and Chief, Division of Behavioral Science, Department of Family and Community Medicine, Southern Illinois University School of Medicine*

SPECIAL 25%-OFF DISCOUNT!

Order a copy of this book with this form or online at:
http://www.haworthpress.com/store/product.asp?sku=4967

BECOMING A FORGIVING PERSON

A Pastoral Perspective

_____in hardbound at $22.46 (regularly $29.95) (ISBN: 0-7890-1855-1)

_____in softbound at $11.21 (regularly $14.95) (ISBN: 0-7890-1856-X)

Or order online and use special offer code HEC25 in the shopping cart.

COST OF BOOKS_____

OUTSIDE US/CANADA/
MEXICO: ADD 20%_____

POSTAGE & HANDLING_____
*(US: $5.00 for first book & $2.00
for each additional book)*
*(Outside US: $6.00 for first book
& $2.00 for each additional book)*

SUBTOTAL_____

IN CANADA: ADD 7% GST_____

STATE TAX_____
*(NY, OH, MN, CA, IN, & SD residents,
add appropriate local sales tax)*

FINAL TOTAL_____
*(If paying in Canadian funds,
convert using the current
exchange rate, UNESCO
coupons welcome)*

☐ **BILL ME LATER:** ($5 service charge will be added)
(Bill-me option is good on US/Canada/Mexico orders only;
not good to jobbers, wholesalers, or subscription agencies.)

☐ Check here if billing address is different from
shipping address and attach purchase order and
billing address information.

Signature_____

☐ **PAYMENT ENCLOSED:** $_____

☐ **PLEASE CHARGE TO MY CREDIT CARD.**

☐ Visa ☐ MasterCard ☐ AmEx ☐ Discover
☐ Diner's Club ☐ Eurocard ☐ JCB

Account # _____

Exp. Date_____

Signature_____

Prices in US dollars and subject to change without notice.

NAME_____

INSTITUTION_____

ADDRESS_____

CITY_____

STATE/ZIP_____

COUNTRY_____ COUNTY (NY residents only)_____

TEL_____ FAX_____

E-MAIL_____

May we use your e-mail address for confirmations and other types of information? ☐ Yes ☐ No
We appreciate receiving your e-mail address and fax number. Haworth would like to e-mail or fax special
discount offers to you, as a preferred customer. **We will never share, rent, or exchange your e-mail address
or fax number.** We regard such actions as an invasion of your privacy.

Order From Your Local Bookstore or Directly From
The Haworth Press, Inc.
10 Alice Street, Binghamton, New York 13904-1580 • USA
TELEPHONE: 1-800-HAWORTH (1-800-429-6784) / Outside US/Canada: (607) 722-5857
FAX: 1-800-895-0582 / Outside US/Canada: (607) 771-0012
E-mailto: orders@haworthpress.com
PLEASE PHOTOCOPY THIS FORM FOR YOUR PERSONAL USE.
http://www.HaworthPress.com

BOF03